Betsy Brown ♡

MARIONETTES

John Wright's Marionettes: the good fairy Magicia Delisia from *Briar Rose* by Rose Fyleman.
'Take heart dear friends and all will yet be well, for though I cannot lift this cruel spell—this I can do . . .'

THE HOW TO DO IT SERIES NO 43

MARIONETTES

by DONALD SEAGER

THE STUDIO PUBLICATIONS

London & New York

First published 1952

Published in London
by The Studio Ltd., 66 Chandos Place, W.C.2
and in New York City by the Studio Publications Inc., 432 Fourth Avenue.
Printed in England
by William Clowes and Sons, Limited, London and Beccles

CONTENTS

Introduction   6

1 The Nature of Marionettes   8

2 Paper Dolls and Simple Controls   10

3 Animals in Cardboard   18

4 Introducing the Toy Soldier   22

5 Ophelia—a rod puppet   26

6 Techniques in Tape   34

7 From Rags to Beauty   40

8 Casting in Plaster   48

9 An Introduction to Wood Carving   52

10 Carving in the Solid   58

11 Restricted Joints   62

12 Specialities   68

13 A Simple Theatre   74

14 To the Future   79

Bibliography   80

INTRODUCTION

The past quarter-century has seen a vast change in the nature of the marionette art. The marionette has graduated from the fairground to the classroom, has found an honoured place in the Edinburgh Festival and in the affections of all young 'viewers'—for the B.B.C.'s Muffin is one of television's most-loved characters.

This has not happened by accident. Perhaps Mr H. W. Whanslaw began it all with his book *Everybody's Theatre* (Wells Gardner, Darton & Co Ltd, 1924). Certainly this work led to a flood of correspondence from many different countries and may well have been the touchstone of an unsuspected enthusiasm dormant throughout the world.

One practical result was the forming of the British Puppet and Model Theatre Guild in 1925. This organisation made possible the exchange of ideas and techniques on a new scale, and the work has been taken up and developed by other similar bodies. What had previously been the closely guarded secrets of a few professional puppeteers became available to everyone.

It is not surprising that a craft as rich in tradition as the marionette theatre began to find its way into our schools. The jointed puppets found in the tombs of the Pharaohs, the fascinating leather and wooden dolls of Java: these remind us that the appeal of miniature theatres is as old as civilised mankind.

Changes in educational method are sometimes slow. Some schools still resist the intrusion of anything which savours of play rather than work. With these exceptions, marionettes are on the march in the educational world, and the increasing interest shown in this art by progressive educationists is reflected by the inclusion of puppetry as a part of many Training College courses. A well-known puppeteer summed it up when he said to me recently that he thought puppetry was worth its place in any school curriculum purely as a craft. 'But', he added, 'we must not forget the element of magic which puppets and marionettes bring to the child. This is something other crafts cannot offer.'

When I was helping him to prepare exhibits for the 1948 Edinburgh Festival, I could not help becoming increasingly conscious of the universal nature of this 'magic'. Puppets and marionettes made by children and adults from a dozen different countries were stacked in crates around the room, and the opening of each box revealed some new and exciting tribute to the fascination of the puppet art. The message of a thousand fingers seemed to me to be an expression of the universality of mankind. That people of so many different tongues and traditions should send the results of their skill and labour all the way to Britain was a symbol of unity in a disunited world.

In the same way, differences in political ideology seemed unimportant as I sat enthralled at marionette shows in Leningrad and Riga, or as I watched the exquisite performance of Obratsov's rod puppets in the Moscow Puppet Theatre.

In Britain, the Lanchester Marionette Theatre, begun in 1927, perhaps most nearly approaches artistic completeness. From the earliest days of his partnership with Mr Whanslaw in the London Marionette Theatre, Waldo Lanchester has consistently been associated with all that is best in the puppet theatre.

But Waldo Lanchester and his wife, Muriel, are exceptional people, and one cannot but agree with C. S. Forester's contention that the possibilities of the marionette theatre have yet to be fully exploited.

I must be forgiven, therefore, if occasionally throughout this book I seem to address myself particularly to the teacher, because it is in the hands of the new generation of puppeteers that the future of the marionette art will obviously lie. This does not mean that the techniques described here are for school use only: I sincerely hope they will be of help to many people who are interested in making marionettes in their own homes. Neither does this book set out to define the limits of marionette technique. The methods of making them are so numerous that some selection was clearly necessary and much that is useful may well have been excluded.

My aim has been to introduce a fairly wide range of techniques in the hope that everyone will find something to suit his own degree of skill. In so doing, I have endeavoured to grade the skills required in some sort of ascending order. For this reason, the teacher taking marionette activity for the first time may find this book of particular use.

In conclusion, may I thank the many people who have so generously made available to me the results of their experience and skill. This universal unselfishness prevailing among puppeteers is a guarantee that the marionette art can go forward to a future even richer than its long and colourful past.

Especially I should like to thank John Wright for the photograph which forms the basis of the jacket design, Bruno Tublin who made available much of the material of the Educational Puppetry Institute, Manchester, and Arthur Newman for the sketches, from which the diagrams were prepared by Arthur Hundleby.

Donald W. Seager, 1951

I. THE NATURE OF MARIONETTES

A marionette is a puppet controlled by wires or strings.

Mr Punch is a member of the same family, but the puppeteer wears him on the hand. He is, therefore, described as a glove-puppet. Marionettes are essentially string-puppets.

Many people believe the word comes from the French 'mariolette'—a tiny doll made to represent the Virgin. Certainly, throughout history, men have been inspired with the desire to recreate with model figures the simple beauty of the Nativity. It has also been dramatised perhaps more frequently than any other subject.

The marionette theatre may well have its origin in the happy combination of these twin desires—to the scene around the crib being added the semblance of 'life' through the animation of the figures.

In this book you will find the words 'puppet' and 'puppeteer' frequently used. Invariably they refer to that particular type of puppet we know as marionettes and to the men who operate them.

Marionette-making is a fascinating art, and not the least of its fascinations is the extraordinarily wide range of materials which can be used. Paper, cardboard, cloth and wood all make serviceable marionettes when the technique used is adapted to the nature of the material. This means, in turn, a correspondingly wide range of skills which can be usefully employed. The seven-year-old can make pleasing figures from paper or cardboard. At the other extreme, carved wooden marionettes represent a challenge to the most advanced skills.

To those who have used the techniques themselves the amount of detail given may seem more than sufficient. I ask them to bear with me in the hope they will find fresh ideas to help them in the work they are already doing, But for those who have yet to begin, description can hardly be too elaborate, and here I hope that the illustrations will usefully supplement the text.

Marionette-making is only part of the marionette art. Having made your marionettes you will want to clothe them and to make them perform. Here again, puppets are obliging. The controls by which they are operated can range from a single piece of wire or thread to a highly intricate controller with twenty or more strings.

Puppets have one particular quality which you will soon observe. However badly made, each one has a distinct and individual personality.

In setting down the various techniques, I have found individual marionettes, made by the particular method described, clamouring to have their own characteristics included. I must apologise if this fact gives the impression that any technique may only be suited to the particular character described. But each method does produce a

Bruno Tublin with exhibits at the Educational Puppetry Institute Exhibition, Edinburgh Festival 1948.
Photo: Kemsley Newspapers Ltd, Manchester.

marionette with certain general characteristics, and the character of your marionette will often help to decide the technique you will use.

Marionettes can be made to follow the human form more accurately than glove-puppets, but they still retain some of the extravagance and exaggeration of Mr Punch. The heads and hands need to be a little larger than life-size and the legs slightly shortened to give a closer semblance to reality than exact imitation. One could advance quite plausible theories on optics to explain this, but the practical puppeteer, being an artist rather than a scientist, is fortunately content to accept it as fact and design his marionettes accordingly.

The marionette world awaits your inspection. It is time to describe how to make our first and simplest model.

2. PAPER DOLLS AND SIMPLE CONTROLS

DANCER

This lively little figure can be made by very young fingers.

Perhaps we should not call the Dancer a marionette, since we cannot control his movements in detail. His appeal arises from this very factor, and his uninhibited dance when jiggled up and down on the single control string will delight small children.

He is a symbolic figure, and the symbols used closely approach the flat counterparts seen in children's drawings. The head is round, and the features—since they are painted on to the head—have no contour. The limbs have roundness but little characteristic shape. The hands and feet are symbols, pure and extremely simple. Knots can provide the joints.

HOW TO MAKE IT

The materials needed are a pair of scissors, a knitting needle, a bodkin, some thread or thin string, a quantity of wallpaper or other stiff paper, newspaper and some sticking compound.

To make the body, a long strip of paper about $2\frac{1}{2}$ inches wide is used. This is wound tightly round the knitting needle until the required thickness (say 1 inch in diameter) is obtained. The unused paper is cut off and the end stuck down in the same fashion as when making wallpaper beads. The paper rolls can be rolled *around string* (string is easier for young children to manage than thread, and knots better), thus making it unnecessary to thread them with a bodkin.

The limbs, hands and feet are made in the same way. Approximate measurements for an 8-inch marionette are:

All $\frac{1}{4}$-$\frac{1}{2}$ inch thick:	Length in inches		Length in inches
Upper arm	$1\frac{1}{2}$	Upper leg	$1\frac{3}{4}$
Lower arm	1	Lower leg	$1\frac{1}{4}$
Hands	$\frac{1}{2}$	Feet	$\frac{3}{4}$

It is not suggested that children should work from measurements. They will discover satisfying proportions by trial and error. If newspaper is used, good proportions can be obtained by reference to the width of the columns, for example:

Feet—Half column width.

Arms—One column width each part (upper and lower).

Legs—One column width each part.

Body—Two columns width.

When the different parts of the body have been made they are laid out in position. With very young children it is a good idea to have a 'key' marionette drawn to size on a piece of paper so that unidentifiable parts can be checked against it.

Thread a bodkin and fasten the pieces together in the following order. Tie thread round foot—knot, thread lower leg—knot, thread upper leg—now thread remaining upper leg—knot, thread remaining lower leg —knot, tie foot. The two legs are thus on a continuous piece of thread. Leave $\frac{1}{4}$-inch gaps at each joint.

The arms are treated in the same way—tie hand, knot, lower arm—knot, upper arm— upper arm—knot, lower arm—knot, tie hand.

The body is completed by tying new thread between upper legs, threading this through body and knotting round arm thread at point where upper arms meet. Beads can be used to provide the articulation at the main joints. For the head roll a piece of newspaper (about half a sheet) into a ball, and tie securely with string, leaving several inches hanging down. Cover this paper 'core' with several pieces of newspaper about 6 inches square, each piece being pulled down over the core and pinched together at the neck of the puppet. Finish the head with a sheet of brown or white paper (to facilitate painting) and tie securely round the neck. The length of the string should extend below this and is used to tie the head to the rest of the puppet. With a long needle, thread a long string *up* through the head to come out at the top. The marionette is hung up by this main thread. The base of the neck can be trimmed with scissors.

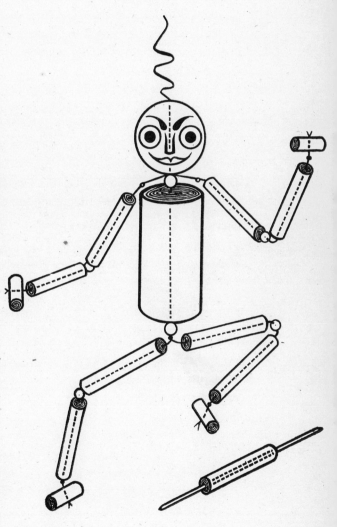

| A simple dancing figure in rolled paper.

11

Simple features may be painted on, remembering that all marionettes are actors and their colouring has the extravagance of an actor's make-up. The eyes, for example, should be heavily underlined in blue. The lips should be bright red.

This principle of make-up painting applies to all marionettes, particularly those which will appear on a lighted stage.

Figure 1 illustrates details of this simple but pleasing character. No costume is needed.

GOLLIWOG

Although the rolled paper technique is simple enough to be within the scope of very young children, it can also be used to make marionettes suitable for stringing.

The Golliwog illustrated in figure 2 is made in this way.

Very young children may need help in cutting out and sewing the head, although even here nothing complicated is involved. Alternatively, the simpler head described on page 11 may be adapted. In addition to the materials needed for the dancer, you will need twelve small wooden beads, although if no beads are available, knots are quite satisfactory.

Marionettes of this size, 8–10 inches, are sometimes difficult to control. Being light, they tend to be sluggish in movement. If the costume is made from thin material this difficulty is less noticeable, but it is sometimes necessary to add weight by winding strip lead round the paper feet before modelling.

DETAILS OF CONSTRUCTION

The limbs and body, like those of the dancer, are made from rolled paper, but the body is more shapely and mobile. The following rolls are required:

	Number	*Length in inches*		*Number*	*Length in inches*	
TRUNK			**UPPER ARM**	2	2	
One piece of each,	2	$1\frac{1}{2}$	**LOWER ARM**	2	$1\frac{1}{2}$	each
$\frac{1}{2}-\frac{3}{4}$ inch thick,	2	$1\frac{3}{4}$	**UPPER LEG**	2	$2\frac{1}{2}$	$\frac{1}{4}-\frac{1}{2}$
forms the upper body,	2	2	**LOWER LEG**	2	2	inch
the remaining three	1	$2\frac{1}{4}$	**FEET**	2	1	thick
the lower body	1	$2\frac{1}{2}$	**HANDS**	2	1	

Wind the pieces for each section—upper body, lower body, each arm and each leg— on to a separate length of string, and paste each firmly.

Arrange the body sections as shown in the illustration, bind with paper cut to shape, and paste and tie firmly.

Now, inserting beads at joints, tie the legs to each side of lower trunk and tie arms to upper extremity.

Plasticine can be used for modelling the feet, provided they are covered with strips of

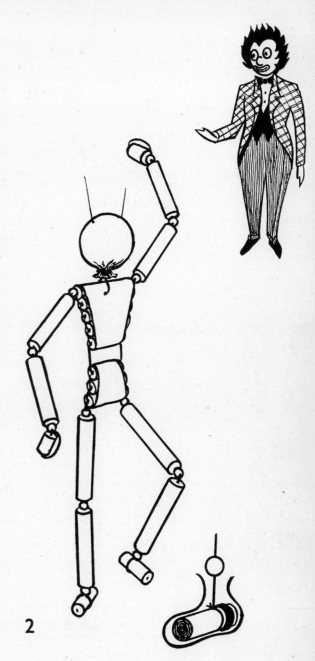

paper or cloth to render them permanent
before painting with tempera or poster
colours. This treatment can also be applied to
the hands.

The Golliwog head is made from an old
black stocking. Stuff the toe with rags until a
round shape approximately 2 inches in
diameter is formed, and tie with thread.

The nose is made by isolating a 'button' of
the stocking with thread. Sew on shoe buttons
for eyes and cut out a piece of bright red or
orange cloth for the mouth; American cloth
is best. More ambitious eyes may be made by
threading a small pearl bead over a black
trouser button. Thread thick black wool into
the head and cut to form the hair. Rug wool
is admirable.

Snip the loose end of stocking off at the
neck, and the head is ready to be fastened to
the rest of the marionette.

To do this, take a long thread, and with a
bodkin push this in through the top of the
head, slightly to one side, bring it out at the
neck, push it through the body below the first
roll and midway between the shoulders, take
it back through the neck and up through the
head slightly to the other side. Knot the
cotton securely to prevent slipping. The loose
ends will be fastened to the head control of
the control bar.

2

An alternative (and probably easier) type
of head for this puppet is made by construct-
ing a basic round head, as described on page
11, and modelling features on it with Plasticine. The whole head is then completely
covered with small pieces of pasted white
paper (the margins of newspapers will do).

13

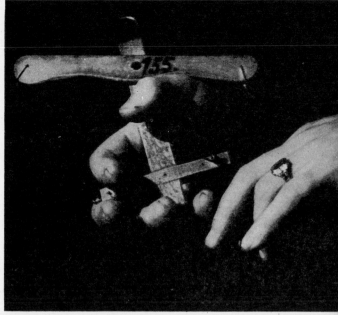

Close-up of the hands of a string-puppet operator at Hans Binter's Marionette Theatre. Photo: H. Gernsheim.

Below: vertical control—simplest for small puppets.

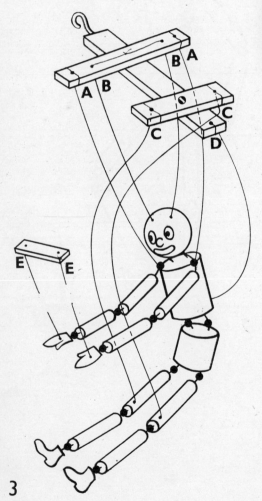

Both of the ends of the string, which have been tied around the paper core, should be allowed to protrude from the neck and these are used to fasten the head to the body.

A SIMPLE CONTROL

The following simple control serves very well with any marionette up to about 10 inches in size. It is made in two parts. Although it does not allow the feet to be moved separately from the legs, this disadvantage is more than offset by its simplicity.

The hand control is very simple. It consists of a wooden rod 3–4 inches long to which the strings from the hands are fastened, one at each end. Make the strings long enough for convenient handling of the marionette. The other strings go to the main control or 'cruciform'. This is made from three pieces of wood strip ($\frac{1}{2} \times \frac{1}{4}$ inch). The main piece needs to be at least 6 inches long, and has a small hook screwed in

3

at one end. This is used for hanging up the marionette when not performing. Across the top of this main piece, nail another piece some 4 inches in length.

You now have a fixed wooden cross. An inch from the base of the cross drill a hole. This should be large enough to take a small bolt if you have one, or to take a piece of stout wire if no bolts are to hand. Drill a corresponding hole in the centre of the remaining crosspiece which should be 2½–3 inches in length. Push the bolt through and fasten to the main piece with a nut or, if wire is used, push this through and bend in the form of a loop at either side. This second crosspiece must be free to swivel.

An even simpler control bar is illustrated in figure 4. It is made of dowel rod and cotton reels bound together with thread and sized for security. Cotton reels should be nicked to ensure firm embedding of the transverse dowels. Use of adhesives will add further strength. A hole drilled in the barrel of each reel to receive a short length of dowel, or a nail driven in, provides a means for fingertip control.

The marionette must be dressed before stringing. The Golliwog costume is quite easy to make, and figure 2 should show sufficient detail. Like all successful marionette costumes, it must be light-weight and loose fitting. Providing these two points are observed, the costume can be just as simple or detailed as skill can make it.

Lay the marionette flat on a table with the control hook away from the body, 3 feet distant. The length of the controls referred to here is suitable for performance on the stage described in chapter 13. Drill a small hole on each side of the main piece about ½ inch from the ends —an awl is the best tool for making the holes in the control bars. Thread the two ends from

The Emperor Charlemagne: Musée de la Vie Wallonne, Liége.

15

the head through these holes from underneath, and knot on top. Now hang up the marionette by the hook of the control bar to complete the stringing.

Thread a needle. Sew into left shoulder and bring thread up to left-hand end of main crosspiece. It should be taut. Loop round the crosspiece, and tie securely. The thread can be prevented from slipping off if small nicks are made in the edge of the crosspiece with a sharp penknife. Repeat with right shoulder.

Thread through costume slightly above left knee and knot at back of knee. Bring this thread up taut in the same way to left-hand end of swivel crosspiece. Treat the right knee in the same way.

Finally, attach a thread from the middle of the back to the end of the main piece of the control, leaving 2–3 inches slack. The marionette is now ready to begin an active life.

It will be noticed that when the main control is held upright all the controls, except that to the back, will be taut. If not, the body will sag and be slow in responding to movements of the control bar.

Hold the main control in the right hand and stand the marionette upright. Keep him upright whilst you practise moving the hands with the other control, which is held in your left hand. Make him raise both arms, now—by tilting the control bar—one arm at a time. Be careful to keep that body upright!

To make your marionette bow, tilt the main control forward slightly. The tension will move to the back string, and the slackening of the head and shoulder controls allows the trunk to bend forward.

Walking will need much practice, but the swivel crosspiece helps. First try moving your marionette smoothly over the floor without attempting to move the legs. Have you managed that? Now, this time—as you move the marionette forward—oscillate the control gently from side to side until those knees begin to pick up.

Finally, try moving the arms at the same time. Take it slowly at first and don't be disappointed if Master Golliwog walks rather like a lame crab at first. Continual practice will bring the marionette's movements more and more into harmony with your own.

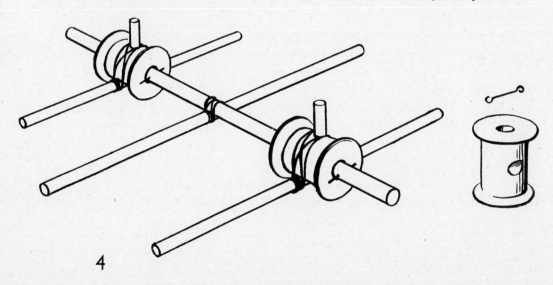

Mrs. M. E. Boardman's puppets: two young dancers demonstrate their miniature counterparts.
Photo: Kemsley Newspapers Ltd., Manchester.

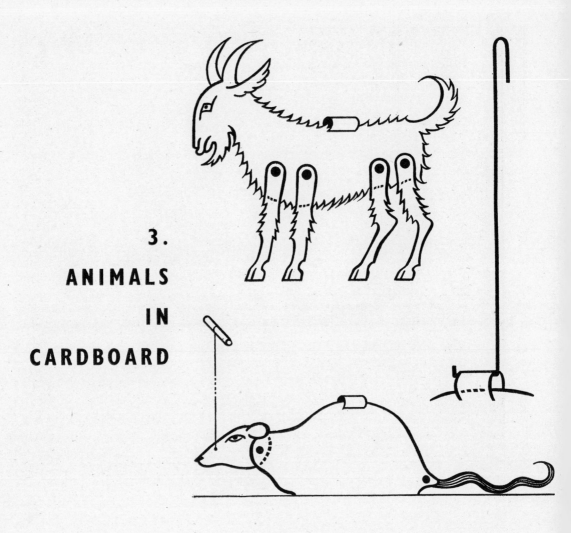

3.

ANIMALS

IN

CARDBOARD

5 Goat and mouse controlled by a stiff wire rod.

Childhood is the age of phantasy and magic. Tiger Tim's adventures may seem a little too fantastic to the adult, and the twelve-year-old may well say, 'Who ever heard of an elephant talking?' But, happily perhaps, the young child is content with a world in which tigers wear trousers and bears argue with boys. Not surprisingly, animal marionettes have a particular fascination for him, a fascination which adults can share in part only.

Animal marionettes are easy to make, and I have seen some charming little figures of lions, dogs and goats made by seven-year-old Flemish children.

The simplest types are made from cardboard. The body shape is drawn on a piece of cardboard and cut out with scissors. The legs are cut separately and fastened loosely

18

R. Bruce Inverarity: gnome and dog from *Hansel and Gretel*. Note the simple means of controlling legs, ears and jaw. Photo: McClintock, Seattle.

to the body with paper-fasteners of the pierce-through type—all four in a row.

An elastic loop is sewn to the top of the animal's back, and when the control—a stiff wire bent at the end—is inserted, the figure can be made to cross the stage with an almost audible clatter of hooves. The goat illustrated in figure 5 is an example of this simple type.

There are possibilities of realistic movement even with such elementary marionettes. A mouse, for example, can have a head made separately from the body and swivelling on a paper-fastener joint. When the control string is lifted, hey presto!—our mouse looks up and takes an interest in his surroundings. His tail is made of string.

On pages 20 and 21 are famous animal characters to inspire further experiment.

20

Annette Mills' famous
television character,
Muffin the Mule.
Copyright:
British Broadcasting Corporation.

Opposite
Jan Malik's two mice
from Hans Anderson's
The Tin Soldier for the puppet
theatre of the Artistic Education
Society, Prague.
Photo: V. Scholz.

Cactus the Camel,
another favourite character from
the B.B.C.'s television programmes.
Copyright:
British Broadcasting Corporation.

Opposite
V. Sucharda: a trio of beetles
from *The Cricket as a Fiddler*
produced in Prague.

4. INTRODUCING THE TOY SOLDIER

This is probably the simplest marionette it is possible to make from wood. It is well within the scope of the eleven-year-old, and can be operated with the type of control described in chapter 2.

You will need a small tenon saw, a $\frac{3}{8}$-inch chisel, some pliers, some paste, glue, small wire nails, dowel rod, newspaper and scraps of silk and tissue paper. Two dozen small screw-eyes will be wanted for the joints.

The 'wooden' movements of the Toy Soldier are well expressed by the wooden limbs of this 12-inch marionette, which is made almost completely from dowel rod of $\frac{3}{8}$-inch diameter. The joints are made from string loops and screw-eyes. The feet can be stiff or mobile according to the technique used.

Plasticine and paper are used for the head, which is hollow when completed.

TO MAKE THE HEAD

Figure 6 illustrates the various stages of construction, which are as follows:

A. Take a piece of Plasticine and mould a half-ball shape about $2\frac{1}{2}$ inches long and 2 inches wide. Clay can be used as an alternative, but since the Plasticine is recovered for re-use little expense is saved.

B. Make the eye-holes about one-half of the way down the head, by pressing in with the fingers. Make similar depressions at the ears and at the sides of the neck.

C. Add rolls of Plasticine for the eyebrows, eyes and ears. The nose is made with two blobs of Plasticine either side of a triangular piece which forms the 'bridge'.

D. Stick on a large ball for the chin, a flat piece for the mouth and rolls for the cheeks. Smooth over with a piece of wood or a nail-file, and model until the result pleases you. Aim at a slightly exaggerated effect, since some of the detail will be lost when the Plasticine is covered with paper.

E. Coat this Plasticine mask with vaseline, taking care to grease the ears and eyes particularly well, and cover the whole of the front of the head with pieces of newspaper torn to the size of a shilling. When the first layer is complete, brush the head well with cold-water paste. This is the paste that wallpaper hangers use and can be bought at the ironmonger's in powder form for a few pence. If it is mixed carefully, stirring all the while you add the powder to the water, it will be free from lumps. Now add a further layer of paper, paste, and put on the final covering of paper strip. Allow to dry.

F. When dry, prise this paper mask carefully away from the Plasticine core. Strengthen the edges of the mask with further pieces of pasted paper. It is also advisable to strengthen the features *inside* the mask. To do this, brush the inside of the mask with glue—hot carpenter's glue is best, but Seccotine or Croid will do—and press in small pieces of silk and tissue paper.

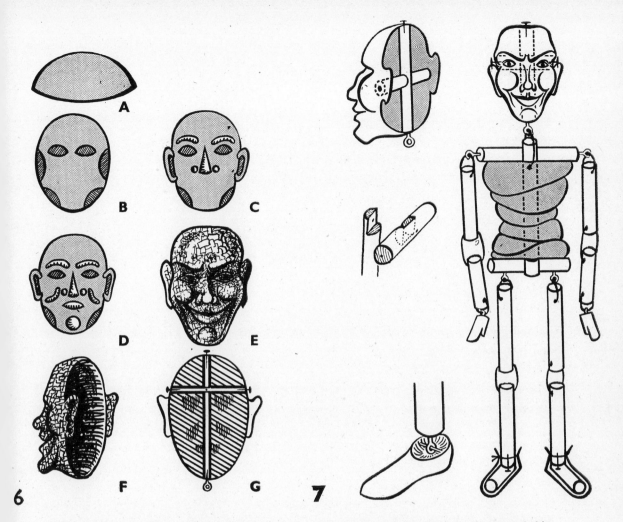

Construction of mask head for the toy soldier. A. clay in half-sphere shape; B. the eyes, ears and chin begin; C. eyebrows, nose and ear details are added; D. mouth, cheeks and chin follow; E. the head covered with torn paper; F. the mask with clay removed; G. the crosspiece fitted.
Figure 7: the soldier assembled from dowel rod. An alternative foot is also shown.

G. This hollow mask is now fitted with a dowel crosspiece: see figures 6 and 7. Using pieces of dowel, measure the width of the head just above the ears, and mark the outside of each piece at the cross joint. Now saw halfway through each dowel at the points marked. Remove the waste wood with the chisel, smear the joints with glue, press together and make secure with a small wire nail. Fix this crosspiece into the mask with small wire nails at top and sides, and with a small screw-eye at the bottom. This will later be used to attach the head to the body.

Stuff the back of the head with paper until a side-view of the head shows a pleasing roundness, and cover completely with a layer of pasted paper strip, taking particular care with the join between mask and paper stuffing.

The head is now ready to be painted. Any appearance of 'roughness' can be put right before painting. Two layers of Alabastine plaster will give a hard, smooth surface.

TO MAKE THE BODY

The body is made on a dowel rod framework and is extremely simple in construction.

Cut pieces of dowel rod of the following approximate lengths:

	Pieces	Length in inches		Pieces	Length in inches
Shoulders	1	3	Hands	2	$\frac{3}{4}$
Spine	1	4	Upper legs	2	$2\frac{1}{2}$
Hips	1	$2\frac{1}{2}$	Lower legs	2	$1\frac{1}{2}$
Upper arms	2	$1\frac{1}{2}$	Feet	2	1
*Lower arms	2	$1\frac{1}{4}$			

Lay the spine across the centre of the shoulder and hip pieces, mark round shoulder and hip pieces with pencil, saw halfway through the dowel down these markings and remove waste wood with chisel.

Saw down the centre of the dowel to a depth of $\frac{3}{8}$ inch. A small vice will be useful here. Now lay the spine flat on a bench or piece of waste wood and, $\frac{3}{8}$ inch from the end, saw down to this first saw cut. One piece of the dowel should now fall away. The flat surface left will fit into the space chiselled out of the hip dowel.

The neck needs to extend approximately $\frac{1}{4}$ inch beyond the shoulders, so cut a piece from the spine, $\frac{3}{8}$ inch wide and $\frac{3}{16}$ inch deep, $\frac{1}{4}$ inch from the opposite end.

Dab glue in these joints, press together and secure with a nail. Cut a piece out of the hands as shown, and the marionette is ready for assembly.

Lay the parts on the bench and fasten all joints with either string loops (threaded through holes drilled in the dowel) or a combination of screw-eye-string-loop as shown in the diagram. When complete except for the head, pad the body out by winding strips of material round the spine as shown in figure 7. The shoulders can be built up with Plasticine, covered with layers of pasted paper.

The Toy Soldier now awaits his uniform: see figure 8. Trousers are fitted first. These are made from black material and have yellow silk piping sewn down the sides. The tunic is of red or scarlet material and made in three pieces. The first piece slips over the neck to hang back and front, and separate pieces are let in at the sides to complete. Small silver buttons are sewn on the chest and the tunic is finished by the addition of yellow silk braiding. The belt is made of American cloth stitched to the tunic.

If you have a suitable metal buckle, this is a useful finishing touch, but cardboard covered with silver paper can be used for this and also for the buttons.

A loose stiff collar of black material should be made to cover the neck joint.

The sleeves are fitted as indicated in figure 8. They should be of similar material to the tunic, and the two separate sleeves stitched together across the shoulders. Epaulets of cardboard with silver paper glued to them will give that final military flourish.

You may make the feet either fixed or flexible. The flexible foot is carved from softwood and is attached to the leg by a wire fastened across the inside of the hollow ankle and passing through the screw-eye from the lower leg. The fixed foot is made by nailing an inch-long piece of dowel to the leg. When covered with a bootee of black American cloth held to the ankle by a drawstring this has quite a finished appearance.

The costume details given here are merely suggestions. Here, as elsewhere, the dressing of your marionette is a splendid opportunity for improvisation and experiment.

To complete the Toy Soldier, make a cardboard pillbox hat one size too large for the head. It is painted black with a red crosspiece. Glue some crêpe hair inside the hat, daub liberally with glue, and push on to the head. Trim the hair to length, and paint on the features with water or powder colours.

The colours of the face can be brightened by giving the painted head a coat of clear shellac or nail varnish.

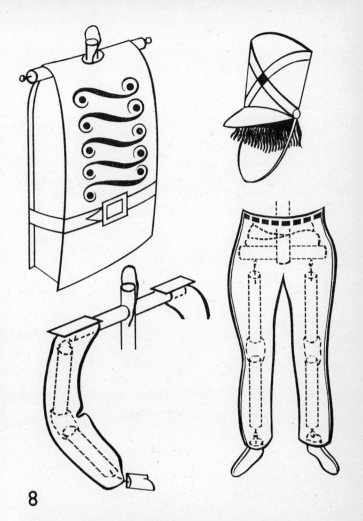

8

Right: Mrs Bickerdike of the Ebor Puppets dressing a puppet: the preparation of the paper patterns. *Above*: costume details of the toy soldier.

5. OPHELIA
A ROD PUPPET

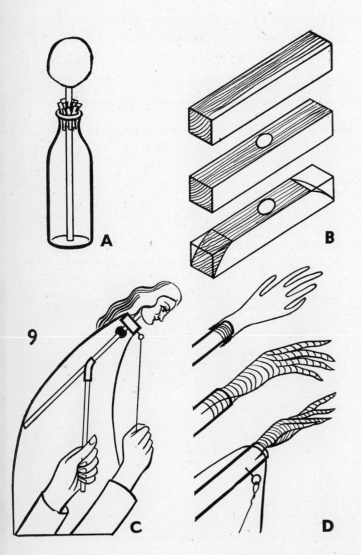

A

B

9

C

D

The tragic Ophelia of Shakespeare's *Hamlet* can be beautifully interpreted through the slender form of a rod puppet. The sensitive control of the hands and head allows superbly fine movements to be made. It is not by accident that Sergei Obratsov, the artistic genius of the Moscow Puppet Theatre, finally selected this type of marionette after years of experiment.

The delicacy of movement of these particular puppets was brought home to me as I sat one January night in that tiny theatre and watched the exquisite motions of the head of the *Reindeer King* in the gifted hands of the Soviet maestro. Here, it seemed to me, the puppet theatre suddenly achieved maturity.

I include a description of such a marionette because I feel no book would be complete without reference to this particular technique. It can be used successfully by children of secondary school age.

The rod puppet is controlled from beneath by rods or stiff wires. Although wire is used most commonly nowadays, the name 'rod puppet' remains to remind us that civilisation existed before galvanised wire. These marionettes perform in the glove-puppet type of theatre where only the head and upper body are seen by the audience. Figures 9 and 10 illustrate the construction details.

THE CONSTRUCTION

Tools and materials needed: 5 feet of $\frac{3}{8}$-inch dowel rod, some Plasticine, a saw, a spokeshave or rasp, a drill,

26

glasspaper, paste, glue, five small screw-eyes, some yellow silk, watercolours, 3 feet of galvanised wire, some copper wire, adhesive tape, a short length of rubber tubing and some thread.

The head is made first, since this will decide the proportions of the shoulders and body. A usual size is from 2 to 3 inches in depth. The dowel rod body should be not less than a foot in length and preferably nearer 15 inches.

Take a piece of ⅜-inch dowel rod 15–18 inches long and drop into an empty bottle, making secure with newspaper. Model a complete Plasticine head on the rod in a similar way to that described in the previous chapter. When the modelling is completed, cover entirely with thin paper pasted over the Plasticine.

The head can conveniently be made from clay rather than Plasticine. It should not be too large because of the weight factor.

Now the shoulders. Take a piece of wood ¾×1×4 inches and shape as shown in figure 9 with a spokeshave or rasp.

Now drill a ½-inch hole through the centre of this block, as shown, and smooth both shoulders and this neck aperture with glasspaper.

On the underside of the shoulder block and ½ inch from each end drill two holes ⅜ inch in diameter. Saw two 1-foot lengths of dowel rod, dip the ends in glue and push into the holes. Allow to dry.

To make the arms, saw two 3-inch

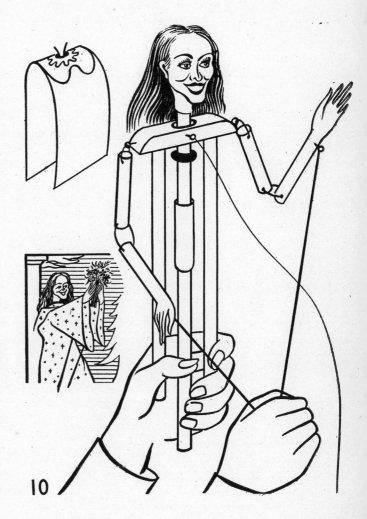

Ophelia in action: and a detail of the simple costume.

Opposite: details of the assembly.
A. Plasticine head ready for modelling; B. stages in making t he shoulder block; C. Ophelia makes a bow; D. development of the hands.

27

1

2

3

4

5

Pantalone, father of Angella and master of the royal hunt.

6

Brigella (a character from the Comedia dell' Arte) pupil of Farfarello.

7

Tartaglio turned into an ugly monster. *Below*: the half-witted steward.

8

The king turned into a hermit. *Below*: a bear from the hunting scene.

9

10

Mary Saunders' puppet 'Ophelia', winner of the Davidson trophy at the Puppet Guild exhibition, 1946.

Opposite: Carlo Gozzi's *Deer King*. King Deramo, desiring to choose a queen, assembles the eligible brides of the court, who arrive escorted by their admirers. Angella, daughter of Pantalone, loves the king ardently and sincerely. But the king is turned into a deer by the magician Farfarello on orders from the evil Tartaglio who schemes to seize the kingdom and the lovely Angella. Now Brigella turns Tartaglio into an ugly monster and the king into a hermit and one of the tragic scenes is Tartaglio's attempt to slay the king. A rod-puppet production of the Moscow Puppet Theatre. Photo: S. C. R.

lengths of dowel rod and two of 2 inches. To these shorter pieces will be fixed the hands, which are made from copper wire bound round the dowel at the wrist, shaped to a slender hand outline and covered carefully with adhesive tape. This type of hand can be bent as required and can be made to hold small articles such as Ophelia's garland of flowers.

Fasten the lower arm to the upper arm, and the upper arm to the shoulder with the string and screw-eye joints shown on page 23. Saw the central dowel rod about 4 inches from the neck, and, after inserting through the neck aperture, reconnect with a short length of rubber tubing. A small collar of lead strip or paper-covered Plasticine should be secured round this dowel about 1 inch below the shoulder block.

It will be found that when the marionette is held by the central dowel, this collar prevents the shoulder block sliding too far down the rod. Attach a length of thread to a screw-eye in front of the shoulder block, and by pulling this thread Ophelia can be made to incline forwards.

To move the head from side to side, hold by the outside rods and rock the central dowel. The head can also be turned by rotating the centre rod.

In practice, I have found that a simplified form of rod puppet performs almost as well as the one described.

In the construction of this simpler model in schools I have found it best to get a few older boys to prepare the rods for the whole group.

To do this, they cut a set of rods each about 18 inches long and a series of wooden strips (cut from one length of wood $1-1\frac{1}{2}$ inch $\times \frac{1}{2}-\frac{3}{4}$ inch). The length of these 'shoulder blocks' can be varied from about 3 to 5 inches, thus allowing each child to select a shoulder width suited to the character he intends to make. The prepared rod has about 2 inches of dowel protruding above the shoulder block.

A small hole is made in the rod just below the shoulder block and a piece of wire is pushed through this hole and wound around the shoulder block to secure it. The rod passes through a hole drilled in the block.

The hands and arms are controlled by 18-inch lengths of galvanised wire bent round screw-eyes screwed into the wrists. Old umbrella ribs make quite satisfactory control rods.

COSTUME

To complete Ophelia, dress in a simple one-piece costume shaped as shown. An effective costume is made from silvered plastic material or balloon-fabric, which hangs straight

Opposite: two scenes from *Der Drachentöter* (*The Dragon Killer*) a puppet pantomime in one act. At the rise of the curtain a princess is discovered guarded by a fearsome dragon. A court official threatens the dragon with banishment if the princess be not released. Since the dragon remains indifferent, the Samurai, a Japanese warrior (above) is sent to kill the reptile, but fails in the attempt. Then Buddha appears (*below*), overcomes the dragon by his divine will, and frees the princess. Rod puppets by Professor Richard Teschner of Vienna. The late Professor Teschner considered the only sound accompaniment appropiate to his wonderful fantasies is a light, tinkling music.

Marjorie Batchelder's Puppet Players. *St George and the Dragon*, rod puppets by Edgar Caper.

without creasing. It is a good idea to fit this before making the collar stop, although it can easily be slit at the neck and stitched up again.

The hair is made from yellow silk thread sewn to a small piece of thin stockinette which is then glued to the top of the head. Tie firmly while drying.

Paint the head and the features in delicate tints, and finish with a coat of shellac to preserve and enhance the colouring. Unless pink adhesive tape has been used, the hands should be painted with pink water-colour.

The sleeves should be very full, particularly at the wrist, so as not to interfere with the control wires, the upper 5–6 inches of which should be covered before the control comes out of the costume below the elbow. The sleeves should be attached to each other across the shoulder block so that they cannot slip down the arm, and are part-secured to the wrist by binding with white cotton. White silk is a suitable material and this can be matched up with a collar and short mantle of the same stuff. Simple embroidery or lace will enhance the simplicity of this costume.

Ophelia is but one example of a marionette in this style. I hope that the pleasure which this creation may give will lead to further experiments with rod puppets. Tradition and experience show them to be matured exponents of the marionette art.

Marjorie Batchelder, Ohio: St. Peter, a rod-puppet for a
dramatisation of a dog story *Moses* by Walter Edmonds.

A character from the Anglo-Austrian Puppet Theatre.
The fixed-rod-body has been combined with string
controls.

6.

TECHNIQUES

IN TAPE

The marionette described in this chapter should be of particular interest to the woodwork enthusiast. Master Box, the first one, is simple enough for the ten-year-old to put together, although the assistance of someone who can handle a saw may be needed to cut out the various parts of the body.

If I may offer a suggestion to handwork teachers, here is a useful way in which scrap softwood may be put to use. Senior pupils, given the measurements, can cut out sets of pieces for the younger boys.

CONSTRUCTION

Master Box is made from wooden blocks glued either side of tapes which form the joints. For the legs, arms and hands, wood strip of dimensions $\frac{1}{2} \times \frac{1}{4}$ inch is admirable, but the other parts of the body will probably need to be cut specially.

The following special pieces will be needed for a 10-inch marionette:

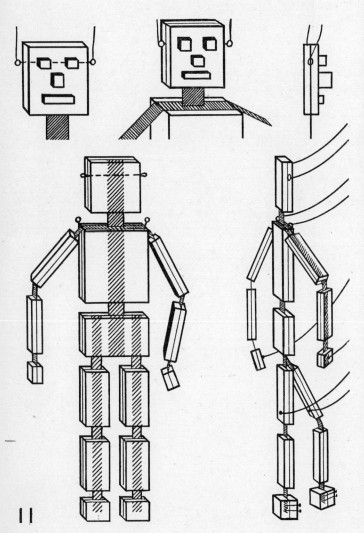

	Pieces	Dimensions
Head	2	$1\frac{1}{2} \times 1\frac{1}{2} \times \frac{1}{4}$ inches
Upper trunk	2	$2 \times 2 \times \frac{1}{4}$ inches
Lower trunk	2	$2 \times 1\frac{1}{2} \times \frac{1}{4}$ inches
Feet	2	$\frac{1}{2}$ inch square

Cut these pieces to size, and saw off the following lengths from wood strip :

	Pieces	Length
Upper legs	4	2 inches
Upper arms	4	$1\frac{3}{4}$ inches
Lower legs and arms	8	$1\frac{1}{2}$ inches
Hands	4	$\frac{3}{4}$ inch

11

Arrange the pieces flat on the bench in the form of the body.

The only other items needed are a length of $\frac{3}{4}$-inch tape, a length of $\frac{1}{4}$-inch tape, a little wire and two screw-eyes.

The upper trunk and lower trunk pieces are glued together with $\frac{3}{4}$-inch tape down the centre, taking care before gluing the lower trunk to insert also the $\frac{1}{4}$-inch tapes. Leave $\frac{1}{4}-\frac{1}{2}$ inch of tape between joints.

Now glue the upper and lower legs with the tape between them. Make a small saw-cut half-way through the foot blocks and, cutting off the tape to within $\frac{1}{2}$ inch of the legs, press into the saw cuts with a knife blade. Secure by driving through small dowel pins. Lay the body under pressure until the glue hardens.

Take a piece of $\frac{1}{4}$-inch tape $11\frac{1}{2}$ inches long, double it over from end to end exactly and make a small slit lengthwise by cutting at right angles to the fold with scissors, Through this slit thread the $\frac{3}{4}$-inch tape. Lay the arm tape flat across the shoulders and leaving suitable gaps between each part, glue on the arms and hands. A layer of glue across the shoulders secures the tape to the upper trunk. Lay aside under pressure for the glue to set.

Finally, fasten the head over the tape. Glue a piece of twisted wire between the wooden blocks as shown. This is made easier if one of them is grooved with a saw cut. The protruding loops take the control strings. Glue small pieces of wood to the face for features.

The marionette is strung as shown in figure 11, the threads going to screw-eyes at the shoulders, and at the hands and knees through small holes drilled in the wood strip and knotted on the reverse side.

This little fellow is ultra-symbolic and has characteristics all his own. When fitted with the type of control described earlier, he is a very valuable practice model. The fact that he wears no clothes is an advantage because the movements of the limbs can be observed in detail, and control improved.

If necessary, nail strip lead to the soles of the feet to add weight.

The wood can be painted or left natural, as desired. If painted, keep the effect simple and bright. Although clothes are not necessary and may not even be desirable, they *can* put a blank, egg-faced figure completely in character. Again, keep the colours and main lines clear and bright, and exaggerate the details.

There are few manœuvres which Master Box cannot perform in the hands of a prac-tised operator, and, if well made, he will outlive several generations of young puppeteers. In weight and 'feel' he comes nearest, of all those made by simple techniques, to the really professional puppet. Refinements of jointing and facial expression are lacking but this will only serve to encourage the novice to further efforts. In the meantime the possibilities of Master Box, or of his slightly refined brother, the Genie of the Lamp, should be fully explored.

THE GENIE OF THE LAMP

This is a slightly more ambitious example of the same technique. A greater attempt is made at accurate representation, and the use of costume covers any small defects remaining. The head, as with most marionettes, is the key to success, and time spent in modelling this is well repaid.

So far in this book we have made allowance for the limitations of young fingers and avoided difficult techniques. Although papier mâché, with which the Genie's head is best made, is not as complicated as it may sound, its use does involve considerable preparation, and children of primary school age may find it a little beyond them. It is such a grand method of making heads for stringed marionettes, however, that I would strongly recommend its use.

Papier mâché can be used for very simple heads, but, at the same time, it has potentialities rich enough to find favour with professional artists of the marionette theatre.

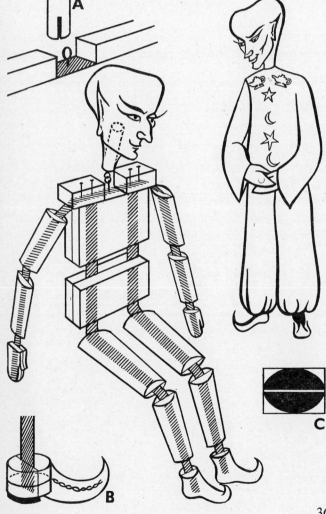

THE PAPIER MÂCHÉ HEAD

To make a head for a 12-inch marionette such as the Genie, you will need two or three newspapers. Tear into small pieces and leave to soak in water for several days, stirring from time to time. Break the soaked paper as small as possible by rubbing over a kitchen grater or between the hands. Continue until you have a soggy grey mixture in which individual pieces of paper cannot be seen.

Now pour this into a clean cloth bag and squeeze out all the water. Mix a quantity of cold-water paste and add the paper pulp to it, stirring all the while. A small quantity of builder's size will bind the mixture more firmly.

You should now have a grey mass of the consistency of wet clay. It should be soft enough to model but not so soft as

The Genie of the Lamp: A. a useful tool for fastening screw-eyes; B. foot detail; C. rounded limbs save wear on costume.

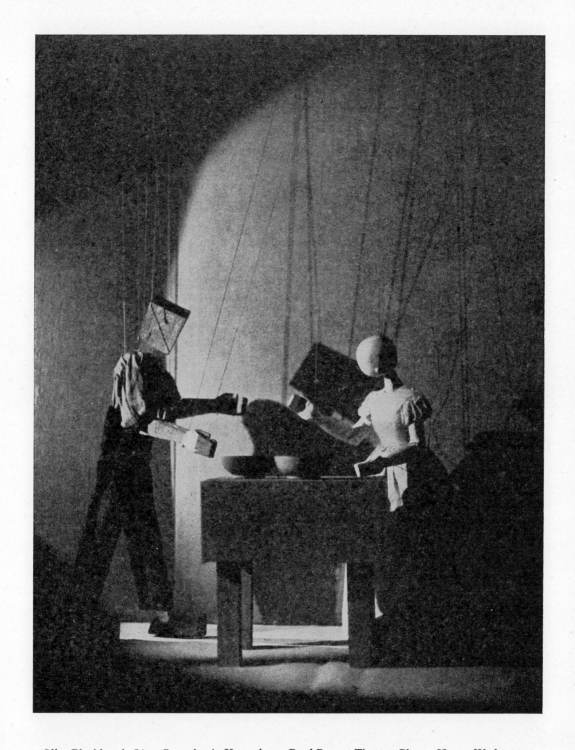

Olive Blackham's *Lima Beans* by A. Kreymborg. Roel Puppet Theatre. Photo: H. van Wadenoyen.

Olive Blackham's Pierrot and Columbine achieve an interesting contrast in shapes. Roel Puppet
Theatre. Photo: Jean Pieters, Paris.

to lose its shape when a piece is laid flat on the work table. If too wet, add more paper
pulp. To moisten, add more paste.

Take a longish piece of dowel rod and make firm in a vice, or slip into an empty
bottle as described in chapter 5. It is a good idea to prepare the head to take the
controls by fastening wire to the dowel rod *before* modelling the papier mâché.
Around the top of the dowel place a piece of papier mâché about 3 inches in diameter,
covering the top inch or so of dowel. Using the fingers, model the head to shape.
Beware of the tendency to leave the back of the head flat. Finish off the fine details,
including the hair, with the aid of a nail-file or piece of wood of similar shape, and
allow to dry in a warm airy place.

When the head is thoroughly dry, any cracks should be plugged with tissue paper
and glue, and the whole head smoothed over with fine glasspaper, which can also be
used to bring out any features inadequately modelled.

Oil colours are best for painting the head.

While the head is drying, you can turn your attention to the body, the size of which
is determined by the finished size of the papier mâché head.

THE BODY

I will not attempt to give exact dimensions for the body but would refer you to the notes on proportion in the first chapter of this book, and figure 12, from which you can readily work out your own measurements.

The trunk, legs and feet are on two continuous tapes, glued between identical pieces of wood. The trunk is jointed at the waist and all edges smoothed down with glasspaper. The legs and arms are rounded after gluing (inset figure 12C).

ARMS AND FEET

The hands are shaped roughly before fastening the tape, and can afterwards be improved with the aid of glasspaper.

To make the feet, saw $\frac{1}{2}$ inch down the centre of a piece of dowel rod, and then across, leaving two $\frac{1}{2}$-inch long half-sections of rod. Tape is glued between them and a piece of wire bound round the outside, continuing away from the dowel about an inch. The rest of the foot is modelled to the dowel on this wire, using either papier mâché or Gesso paste. A piece of lead nailed at the heel will restore the balance of the foot, which should have a hinge short enough to prevent a complete downward swing.

After assembling and cutting off the unwanted tape, the feet and hands are painted with oil colours.

ASSEMBLY

To fasten the arms, first glue a piece of $\frac{3}{8}$-inch tape across the shoulders. Cut a piece of wood $\frac{3}{4}$ inch wide and of body thickness to fit exactly across the shoulders. Saw in half crossways and, leaving a half-inch gap at the centre, glue and nail each piece to the top of the shoulders. The gap at the centre will take the neck of the papier mâché head in such a way that it is prevented from moving too freely from side to side.

To complete the Genie, glue the arms and hands to the tape. Insert a screw-eye in the neck aperture of the body, saw off the head dowel to within $\frac{1}{2}$ inch of the head, and link to the body with a further screw-eye or with a screw-eye-string-loop joint.

A useful and very simple tool for fastening screw-eyes into neck apertures such as this is made from a dowel rod with a short saw cut down the centre, see figure 12. With this particular model, it is easier if you can remember to insert the screw-eye before building up the shoulders, but in other cases this may be impossible.

The Genie is now ready to be dressed. Any degree of plumpness may be obtained by winding old material round the body—avoiding the joints—and nailing into place. A suggested design for a silk costume is shown in figure 12.

If the parts of your marionette body are well smoothed over with glasspaper, such a costume will have quite a long life.

The controls, fastened to the upright control bar recommended for small marionettes are secured by piercing the costume and marionette, and knotting on the reverse side.

39

7. FROM RAGS TO BEAUTY

In this chapter are described two different ways of making marionettes with heads of cloth and paper.

Both the Clown and Red Riding Hood have paper and cloth masks incorporated in the heads, but the two techniques are quite distinct.

In presenting these two marionettes, I do not suggest that the twelve-year-old child would find them easy to make unaided. I am sure, however, that there is nothing in their construction beyond a child of this age. Pupils of the Moseley Junior Art School, Birmingham, for example, have, with the advice of their teacher, Miss Truda Lane, made marionettes like these in their own homes and I know this success to be shared by many other teachers.

Adult fingers may be quicker, however, and, particularly with the Clown, a sewing machine will save much time, but as you will appreciate when you come to make them yourself, there is really nothing difficult about these seemingly complex dolls.

First, the matter of size. Rag bodies are light; therefore they need to be large if you want a vigorous marionette. Anything smaller than 12 inches is difficult; 15 inches is probably the best size to aim at. These larger marionettes need a bigger type of control, and this chapter is, therefore, chosen to introduce the horizontal control bar.

ENTER THE CLOWN

The Clown is a simple general-purpose marionette and his rag body has a flexibility well in keeping with his character.

His head is made as illustrated in figure 13. It begins as a tight ball of newspaper tied with string, A. Over this is modelled a suitable face in Plasticine, B, and this is covered with paper. C shows how a strip of strong cloth is glued to the head, and D the way in which the covering is completed by pasting paper strips over the back of the head.

When the cloth strip is joined under the chin, E, this makes a loop by which the body will be attached to the head. A frilly collar, F, neatly covers the join.

Alternatively, the construction described on page 43 can be adapted for use with models for whom a frilly collar would be unsuitable. Finish by modelling features with Plasticine, cover with paper strip and paint.

This marionette has an advantage over the circus clown; he does not need a skull cap to cover his hair because he has none.

The ears and other features are painted, in all their traditional extravagance, using poster colours.

To string the head, thread the control through the cloth strip on one side, and out at the other. Knot either side to prevent slipping.

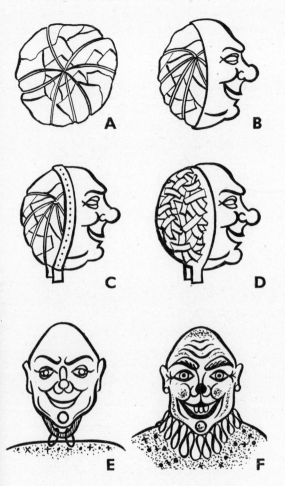

13

The construction of the clown's head: A.
rolled newspaper; B. mask modelled from
Plasticine; C. when covered with paper,
attach cloth strip; D. back of head completed; E. cloth strip joined and attached
to body; F. a frilly collar covers the join.

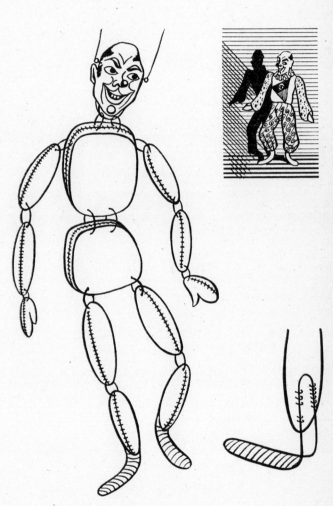

14

The clown: body construction. *Bottom
right*: how wire foot-frame is attached to
cloth leg.

41

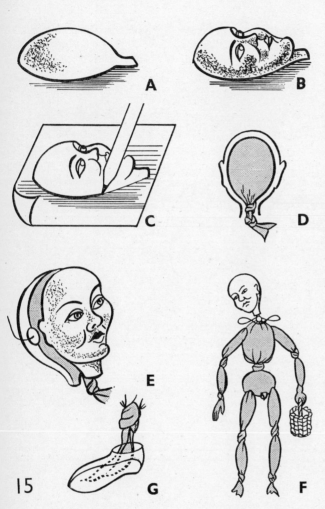

Red Riding Hood: points of technique. A. neck is included in original head shape; B. facial details added; C. tracing an outline for back of head; D. how head and body are joined; E. fastening felt pads; F. the complete body; G. foot detail

To make the body, including the hands, first draw a rough design (front-view) on paper. Enlarge to a size proportionate to the head and use the paper pattern to cut out two pieces of old dress material or shirting to each part. Sew up three sides of the body pieces, leaving an aperture in the narrowest side. Turn inside out, stuff lightly with cotton waste or cut-up rag, and the body is ready for assembly.

The best way to stuff the arms and legs is with rolled pieces of paper. These ensure stiffness. To obtain additional weight, roll strip lead inside the newspaper stuffing.

The feet are made with an open wire frame (as shown in figure 14), and covered with black adhesive tape. This gives the clown a pair of long flat shoes.

Long loop-stitches are used to joint the body pieces together and it is an easy matter to fit the costume—see illustration—by sewing it direct to the body.

In making other characters with this same technique, it is worth bearing in mind that wash-leather is an excellent material for hands, and that if a flesh-coloured head is required you can do no better than to glue strips of old silk stocking over the finished mask.

RED RIDING HOOD

This 12- to 15-inch marionette has a conveniently simple attachment between head and body which depends upon making a paper head in two separate halves. These are afterwards joined together with a stuffed stocking head between them.

First, you take a piece of Plasticine sufficient to make a half-head about $3\frac{1}{2}$ inches in diameter. Press this down on a piece

16 A suggested costume for Red Riding Hood:
light woollen or cotton is the most suitable material.

Professor Harro Siegel: a Spanish dancer.
Photo: R. Kruger, Berlin.

of flat board, and model a neck about $\frac{3}{4}$ inch in length, as in figure 15A. The facial details are built up in Plasticine, the mask covered with Vaseline, and three or four layers of paper strip pasted over it.

When dry, remove with a penknife and trim the edge with a pair of scissors. Lay flat on a piece of paper and trace the outline accurately in pencil, C. This tracing is used as a base on which you model the back of the head in Plasticine and cover similarly with paper strip. When dry, prise this paper shell from the back of the head and trim the edge to fit flush with the edge of the face mask. Strengthen the inside of each section of the head with glue and rag.

Find an old silk stocking and darn any holes before commencing to make the body. Stuff the toe with cut-rag or cotton waste until you have a shape which will just fit into

Eric Bramall: a Spanish dancer in the ballet *Dance Fantasy*

the hollow mask. Now knot the stocking and close the two halves over the stuffed section.

Secure the halves together with pasted paper strip and cover the whole head with a fresh layer of paper. Glue a small round felt pad above each ear before threading the head control through the head with a large needle. The control should enter through one pad and come out at the centre of the other. The pads will be found useful in resisting the tendency of the paper to tear.

The body is completed by stuffing the stocking, and knotting to form, in turn, the upper and lower trunks. If, when you come to dress Red Riding Hood, you feel the shoulders are not sufficiently prominent, slip a piece of stout wire shaped like an elongated figure eight over the upper trunk and twist the wire to make secure at the neck join. Arms and legs are made from tubes of stockinette stuffed in the same way as the Clown's.

The hands can be made with copper wire covered with stockinette and loosely padded. One of these hands can easily be bent to hold the wire and raffia basket.

You make the feet separately with a piece of wire shaped to the sole of the foot, over which is sewn a piece of black American cloth in the shape of a boot. This is padded out with cotton waste, the loose end of stockinette from the leg sewn inside the upper part, and, when the foot has been adjusted to hang neatly, the back of the shoe is stitched to this same piece of stockinette.

The arms and legs are stitched to the body with long stitches, and after painting the head in water colours or tempera, with a final gloss-over of shellac, fasten some blonde crêpe hair. The marionette now only needs a costume such as suggested in figure 16 to complete her character. The under-skirt should be preferably of a darker material. It can be long, as shown in the figure, or finish at the knee, in which case, the legs and hands, being made from stockinette, give quite a natural appearance.

CONTROL FOR LARGE MARIONETTES

Types of control are almost infinite in their variety. Nearly all puppeteers have their own particular variations around a basic pattern. Some, like Waldo Lanchester, creator of the delightful Lanchester Puppets, seem to prefer the vertical control, even with the largest puppets.

In brief, there is no such thing as a standard control. Any control which allows you to work your marionettes easily and completely is a good control, and, whereas there is much to be said for the vertical control in the professional marionette theatre, I believe that the horizontal type described here will prove more suitable for the beginner who may merely wish to walk his doll across the drawing room carpet or perform with it in an improvised theatre.

For marionettes of 12 inches or larger I would strongly recommend this type.

45

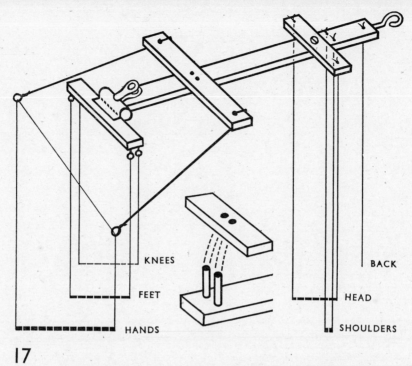

KNEES

FEET

HANDS

BACK

HEAD

SHOULDERS

17

An eleven-string controller, and an alternative to the Bulldog clip.

It is based on a wooden cruciform and has a total of 11 strings which allow quite complicated movements to be carried out. The cruciform is some 10–12 inches long and made from wood about an inch wide and $\frac{1}{2}$ inch in thickness. The upper crosspiece is about 7 inches long and nailed to the main member. A piece of galvanised wire with a loop at the end is pushed through a hole drilled at each end and bent to hang slightly in front of and below the end of the main piece. The control for the hands is threaded through the wire loops before attaching to the marionette. Allow a few inches of slack so that the hands will hang naturally by the sides when the marionette is supported by the head strings.

The head strings are fastened to the ends of the shorter crosspiece which is attached to the centre piece by means of a short, round bolt, which allows it to be swivelled when necessary.

The shoulder strings are threaded and knotted through the main piece close to the head control. The strings should be just slack when the marionette is supported by the head. A slight forward tilting of the control will transfer the weight of the marionette body to the shoulder strings and allow the head to be moved freely with the head strings.

At the end of the main piece, thread a string to the middle of the marionette's back. This will support him when the control is tilted forward to allow the head and shoulders to fall at the beginning of his introductory bow. A large hook, by which the marionette will hang when not in use, is screwed in at this end.

The legs are fastened to a separate control stick which is attached to the main control by means of a Bulldog clip, or with pegs, as shown in figure 17. The object of this detachable fitting is so that the leg control may be operated separately when the marionette is walking or dancing. Single leg movements may be carried out by pulling the strings with the leg control clipped in position. Each end of the leg control takes two strings— the front one to the feet and the rear to the upper knee. They should be slightly slack.

To make your marionette walk, grasp the main control between the two crosspieces, with the hand opposite to the direction in which the doll is to walk, and, taking the leg control in the free hand, detach and slip out under the hand string. This control leads the marionette in the direction of the walk. Twist the control forward so that the foot string hangs loose. Raise one end to lift the knee, and as you move it forward, give the control a slight flick back to its original position, thus bringing the foot forward. Repeat with the other leg.

Perhaps the most difficult part is the co-ordination of your hands, for as the marionette's legs are moved forward, your other hand must bring the main control smoothly across to keep up with them. You will need to practise until you can walk your marionette equally well in either direction.

The hands can be raised together by pucking up the control string between the side wires, and singly by lifting at either side. The knees and feet may be raised either together or singly in a similar fashion.

Practice with this type of control will enable you to carry out almost any reasonable movements. For special movements and effects, the marionette will need additional strings. Some of these are described in the chapter on Specialities.

Some of Waldo Lanchester's string puppets: Baldo and Belso the copper-coloured clowns; Bill the Bo's'n; Clown.

Eric Bramall's head of Faustus.

8. CASTING IN PLASTER

Each completed marionette so far described has introduced fresh techniques.

It will be appreciated that there are literally dozens of different ways of making the various parts of a marionette body. This wide choice, in turn, allows many hundred different combinations of head, body, hands and feet.

Among the main factors in determining which method is best are the degree of skill of the puppeteer, the 'character' of the marionette you wish to make, and the materials most easily obtained.

Limited skill may be due to either lack of previous experience with marionettes or to the physical inability of very young fingers to perform the complex. In either case, the earlier models in this book will commend themselves. Again, choice of technique will tend to depend upon sex. The stuffed rag body, whilst an easy proposition for feminine fingers, may well leave the poor male sighing for chisel and hammer.

The experienced marionette artist will almost certainly determine his choice of technique in the light of the character he wishes to interpret. He will consider what sort of effect he wishes to achieve and choose his materials to bring this out to the full.

For the beginner, perhaps, it is best to consider what materials are to hand, what skills are available and to concentrate on methods which make best use of both.

All of which is by way of apology for this chapter which describes how to make a marionette head in a plaster mould but which omits to describe the body to go with it.

The answer is that this type of head can be used with any type of marionette body. In describing how to make it, too, I am perhaps looking ahead to the carved wooden bodies described later in this book.

Making heads in plaster moulds is fascinating work and, once you are familiar with the technique, it is by no means difficult.

MODELLING THE HEAD

You first need to model a head in Plasticine or clay approximately one-fifth of the size of the body visualised. Make it on a short length of dowel rod of neck thickness and, when modelled to your satisfaction, liberally coat with Vaseline. Since this is to prevent the mould from sticking to the cast head, particular care should be taken to grease all crevices.

Pour a cupful of water into a mixing bowl and slowly feed about three cupfuls of superfine white plaster of Paris into it. The plaster should be crumbled between the fingers to avoid lumpiness, and the whole mixture stirred constantly. It should be of the consistency of thick cream.

Proceed with the next stage as quickly as possible, since the plaster hardens very rapidly.

Take a cardboard box at least an inch larger in all dimensions than the head, and fill to a depth of about 4 inches with plaster, pressing with the fingers to remove any air bubbles. Place the model in the plaster, face upwards, and push down until about half-immersed, preferably leaving the ears uncovered.

Allow to set hard. This should take about an hour.

When the mould has set, treat the exposed half of the plaster with Vaseline to prevent it sticking to the second half of the cast. Prepare a further quantity of plaster and pour gently over the upturned face of the model, covering the highest point by at least one inch. Put aside to harden.

When thoroughly set, tear away the cardboard box and carefully separate the two halves of the mould with a flat knife-blade. Remove the Plasticine, which can be returned to stock for further use.

The mould is now ready for casting heads. I stress the plural because many puppeteers like to cast a set of standard heads from the same mould and develop individual characters afterwards with glasspaper and paints. These cast heads will be found to have a well-rounded effect and are thus particularly suitable for the female marionette.

The heads may be made either with papier mâché, prepared as described in chapter 6, or with plastic wood. Papier mâché is, of course, cheaper, but must not be used too moist as it shrinks considerably. Grease the moulds with Vaseline and press the selected material into the separated halves, aiming at a thickness of about $\frac{1}{4}$ inch. Make sure the material is pressed well down into the features, and allow to extend slightly beyond the edge of the mould. This will take up the natural shrinkage on drying.

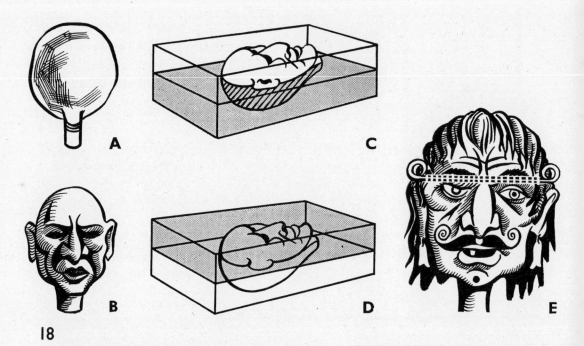

Stages in casting the plaster head: A. clay modelled on to neck; B. feature details added; C. clay head pushed into plaster; D. second half of the mould made by pouring plaster over upturned face; E. finished head.

When thoroughly dry, remove the casts, and place together with a length of wire between them just above the ears. Press together, and smear the seam thoroughly with fresh papier mâché or plastic wood. If papier mâché is used, it is as well to glue the seam first before doing this.

The ends of the wire are bent into loops to take the head strings, and the head finished off by smoothing down with glasspaper. It is then ready for painting. Oil colours are best.

The hair is best modelled on the head before casting, but plastic wood squeezed direct from the tube makes splendid curls, and crêpe hair, string, raffia, wool, or coiled paper strip can also be used.

For attachment to a rag body such as Red Riding Hood's, the wire for the head control should be passed through the stuffed stocking head before joining the two halves of the mask together.

When a wooden body is used, the neck aperture is best plugged with papier mâché or plastic wood, and the joint to the body made with screw-eyes. This arrangement can also be used with the jointed wooden bodies described later in this book.

Figure 18 illustrates several of the stages in making the plaster head.

50

Gerald Shaw: the Bo's'n from *The Tempest*. The Roel Puppets: courtesy Olive Blackham.

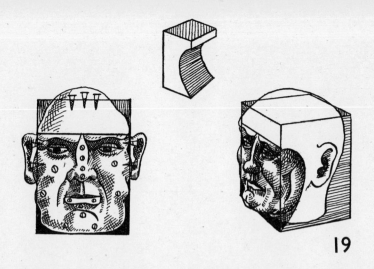

19

9. AN INTRODUCTION TO WOOD CARVING

There is little doubt that wood is the best material for marionette heads and the material which allows the most lifelike imitation of the movement of the human body.

It is only fair to stress at the beginning, however, that wood is not an easy material with which to work. Even the craftsman treats it with respect. It is only because he knows so well what can and cannot be done with it that he achieves his high standards. Wood is responsive to skilled hands but it can be a source of despair for the impatient or unskilled.

Its advantages are considerable. Durability is the most obvious. It also has a weightiness which facilitates control. Finally, it can be used to produce heads of a character and quality few other mediums can approach.

In suggesting methods which enable the hard discipline of wood-carving to be tempered by the use of plastic wood, I am thinking particularly of the needs of those who are unaccustomed to using a chisel. I am sure that out of consideration for 'honesty' in the use of materials, many craftsmen would resist any attempt to make things easier by such a combination of techniques. But this seems to be a case of 'half a head is better than none', and while admitting its makeshift nature, I commend to the beginner the use of plastic wood during his apprenticeship in wood carving.

By carving the head in rough from wood and adding details in plastic wood, the limitations of these two materials are largely offset, much time is saved, the cost is relatively low, and the heads are permanent. There are two main techniques.

FIRST METHOD

A solid block of some softwood such as pine is taken—2 × 2 × 3 inches is a suitable size for your first attempt—and the lower part of the face, below eye level, is cut away with a bow saw or fret saw, figure 19.

52

William Simmonds: three puppets designed for a projected puppet version of the play $x=0$ by John Drinkwater.

This leaves a surface too even for the satisfactory application of plastic wood. Accordingly, small screws or nails are fixed at the places where the eyes, nose, cheeks, ears, chin and top of the head will appear, and the plastic wood is modelled around these. Figure 19 should help to make this clear.

Be careful to apply the plastic wood in a series of fairly thin layers each of which should be allowed to dry before proceeding with the next, otherwise subsequent shrinkage will produce cracks. When completely dry, the rest of the head can be trimmed to shape with a sharp penknife, and the whole head smoothed down with glasspaper ready for painting. Oil colours are best, although enamels can be very effective where a glossy surface is required.

AN ALTERNATIVE

This process is one of building up.

Take the block of wood, and carve roughly to shape. Roughen the surfaces, and reinforce the features with layers of plastic wood. This may not be good craftmanship

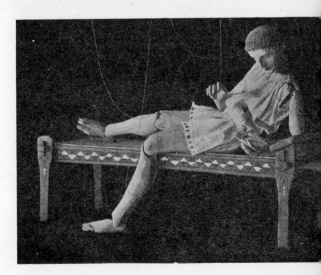

53

but it certainly produces quick results, and plastic wood smeared evenly over the head will also cover any deep or unintentional chisel marks.

Figure 20 gives you an idea of the way in which this type of head is built up.

It is important to make the neck of the marionette sufficiently long to be attached easily to the body.

The neck is probably the most laborious part of the head to carve. You can save work here by drilling a hole in the bottom of the head and gluing in a piece of $\frac{3}{4}$-inch dowel.

It is to be hoped that experience with this method will generate the confidence and desire to attempt a complete carved head. Plastic wood, whilst useful, is nevertheless a prop for the unskilled, and you will never feel quite the same sense of pride in a head doctored in this way as in a successful head carved direct.

But the techniques used in all early marionette work should be simple enough to allow early completion, for only in this way is interest sustained. Heavy complicated work beyond the skill possessed, may result in a loss of interest in the art as a whole.

NEW HEADS—NEW BODIES

Having made your first head in wood, you may feel dissatisfied with the marionette bodies you have so far made. You may well feel that the solidity of the wooden head demands a body which, in turn, is more solid and robust.

The body illustrated in figure 21 has a deep chest and pelvis. It is made as follows:

Two oval pieces are cut from $\frac{1}{4}$–$\frac{1}{2}$ inch thick timber with a bow or fret saw. For a marionette one foot high, they should be about 4 inches wide.

In the centre of one of these ovals, drill a hole with a large bit and wide-sweep brace. Use the method accepted in general woodwork technique, that is, drill until the point of the bit just pierces the opposite side of the wood, reverse, and drill from the other side. This hole is to take the neck of the marionette, which is fitted by means of a screw-eye fastened to a piece of stiff wire let into the underside of the oval across the neck aperture.

The trunk is made from a cloth tube slightly narrower than the widest measurement of the ovals, the tube being stuffed with sawdust and sewn across the centre to form the waist. A *further* cloth tube is fitted round the stuffed body and joined to it by sewing across the central cloth hinge. It is by means of this outer cover that the trunk is attached to the ovals. It is pulled down over each oval in turn, and either glued or fastened with brads, according to the texture of the cloth used and the weight of the marionette. This should be quite clear from the illustration.

The result is a good trunk with prominent hips and shoulders.

The arms and legs are fastened to the ovals with cloth pieces tacked so that the hinge works most naturally forwards and backwards. They may be of stuffed cloth, or you might care to attempt some of the more ambitious limbs described in chapter 11.

20

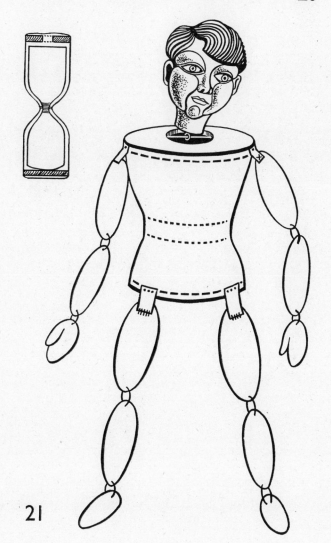

21

John Wright's Marionettes: a production of *Briar Rose* by Rose Fyleman. Two princes, Silly Billy and Willy Nilly, in the enchanted forest which surrounds the castle on the hill of dreams.

V. Sucharda: *The Tale of the Postman* by Karel Capek, produced by V. Surejkal.
Below: Josef Skupa's two famous characters, Spejble and Hurvinek. Photo: V. Heckel

The best way of carving direct from a solid wooden block.

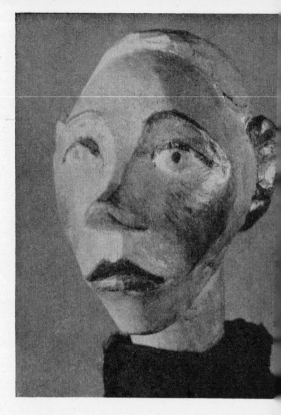

22

10. CARVING IN THE SOLID

BALSA WOOD

Plastic wood should help you to gain the confidence necessary for carving heads in the solid. It can still be used to save heads that might otherwise have to be scrapped because of a slip of the knife or chisel.

But, if you begin with softwood and a penknife before trying your hand at the more difficult technique of chisel-carving, this experience will prove useful in increasing both skill and confidence.

The softer the wood, the less difficult it is to carve. This indicates balsa wood as a first choice.

Used in the construction of model aircraft, it has a strength more than commensurate with weight. Its main disadvantage is that unless suitably weighted by means of lead filling or by attaching a hardwood body it is hardly heavy enough for marionettes. It is also expensive.

Good carving makes the fullest possible use of the initial shape of the wood. For this reason the head is best carved from the original block as illustrated in figure 22.

The Anglo-Austrian Puppet Theatre: the Valet, Sophy and Cassian from *Gallant Cassian* by A. Schnitzler.

The only tools needed are a sharp penknife and some glasspaper.

A block of balsa not less than $3 \times 3 \times 4\frac{1}{2}$ inches, and with the grain running down-wards, will give the best results, the longer section incorporating the neck, which is shaped first. Eye sockets follow. These must be unnaturally deep to allow the nose to assume prominence during later stages of carving.

The mouth and chin are best left until the rest of the head has been shaped. Lines should be as simple and forceful as possible and the head should continually be in-spected from different angles so that an all-round effect is obtained.

Finish off with glasspaper in preparation for painting.

If additional weight is required, bore a hole in the top centre of the head and plug with rolled lead.

PINE AND OTHER SOFTWOODS

With a really sharp knife, the technique does not differ greatly from that used with balsa. There are, however, aids which can speed up the work. The head can be reduced

Franz Zangerle of the Rhineland Marionettes, Cologne, carving the head of a puppet, using a model as a guide for contour and size. Facial characteristics of well-designed puppets invariably appear exaggerated when seen under normal conditions. Transferred, however, to their proper place on the stage, the effects of lighting and distance restore the faces to their true proportions, as they are intended to be seen by the audience.

Below: Max Radestock's heads of Kasperl and a peasant. Note the contrasting character of these two heads.

to the basic shape by placing your block in a vice and sawing off the corners instead of whittling them away. This method has the advantage that the wood does not split along the grain so easily as when a knife is used.

Time may also be saved by working with a wooden cube and fitting a dowel neck afterwards.

The sockets for the eyes can be drilled with a brace and bit in preference to carving. This is both quicker and simpler. When carving with a knife, it is necessary to cut across the fibres, and it is consequently difficult to get a smooth finish in the eye sockets.

The most difficult of all techniques, requiring considerable skill and patience, is that in which hardwood is used. Some notes on the methods most likely to give good results follow.

HARDWOODS

The hardwood head achieves its effect by a pleasing contrast of plane surfaces, just as the appeal of a modelled head lies mainly in the disposition of curved surfaces. I stress this because it may save modellers unnecessary work in trying to make their head of a uniform smoothness. Attempts to disguise the nature of the material used are usually a mistake. Neither should you aim at too detailed or realistic effect. Fine work is lost in the distance which separates marionette from audience, and complete realism in the marionette theatre is, perhaps surprisingly, rarely successful. You should aim rather at caricature, giving your puppet strong characteristics, such as prominent cheekbones, deep-set eyes and interestingly shaped nose and ears.

For work with hardwoods, a chisel and carpenter's vice are essential, and the wood should first be sawn close to size to save carving. You will also need a mallet, a brace and bit, a wood-file and some glasspaper.

Place the roughly-shaped head in the vice. Work first at the forehead and skull, leaving the base of the timber square for as long as possible to facilitate holding in the vice. The chisel should be worked across the grain and never into it, to avoid splitting the wood. A $\frac{3}{4}$ or 1 inch chisel is best.

You will discover the best method of dealing with the features if you study the shape of the head carefully before beginning to use mallet and chisel on those parts where most wood needs to be removed. A curved chisel will be found of great help in shaping the cheeks and chin, and preliminary eye-holes should be bored with brace and bit.

When the chisel has done its best work, use the wood-file to smooth over where necessary, and finish off with glasspaper.

Work in hardwood is not to be recommended except to adults and teen-age boys, since it is both laborious and delicate. The permanence and solidity of the finished model, however, can give very considerable satisfaction.

Where extra-prominent feature details are required, carve them separately, mount on a dowel peg, and joint into the main block.

11. RESTRICTED JOINTS

The ability to carve in wood widens the range of the marionette-maker very considerably. In particular, it enables him to make puppet joints which closely follow the movements of the human body.

By a seeming contradiction, an increase in skill in the making makes a marionette more simple to control. This is because a well-constructed marionette cannot do much wrong even when carelessly handled.

We have dealt previously with joints that were either 'universal', i.e. could bend in all directions, or were only partially restricted. In either case, bad handling of the controls can cause the marionette to take up a grotesquely impossible position, and, while it is sometimes an advantage for our puppets to achieve the seemingly impossible, we do want their actions and their attitudes to bear a close enough semblance to reality to be convincing.

The moment would therefore seem opportune to discuss joints which prevent such disturbing sights as an arm bent backwards at the elbow, or back movements which outrival the contortionist.

BODY JOINTS

The human body, except with the advance of undisciplined middle-age, is able to bend forward to the toe-touching position. The backward movement, however, is very slight. To ensure a similar degree of movement in your marionette, it is necessary to cut away flanges at the middle and lower trunk and to ensure a reasonably flush fit at the back of the body when the marionette is in the normal upright position. Figure 22 illustrates how this may be achieved with a cloth-jointed marionette made from flat wood.

After cutting the trunk pieces and legs to size, the joints are eased by the judicious use of a wood-file. When cloth or leather hinges have been glued into position, the hard edges of the wood are taken off with a piece of glasspaper wrapped round a wooden block.

Kenneth Wood's performing mule. The neck-joint of the mule is unusual in that it is made of a strip of tubular leather belting, the sections of the neck being strung like sections of vertebræ. This gives the neck a flexibility corresponding almost to a universal joint. Photo: Sybil Studios.

Jointing a carved wooden body with cloth hinges. Figure 24: Restricted joints. A, pinned joint; B, leather-hinged joint, and C, cut away leather-hinged joint, both with cotton check.

KNEES AND ELBOWS

Methods of making knee and elbow joints are almost infinite. Figure 24 shows three which have proved very satisfactory. It will be realised that since knee and elbow movements are almost identical, any method suited to one can almost certainly be adapted to suit the other.

The first joint is made by cutting a tenon with rounded shoulders on the upper part of the lower leg. This fits into an open 'mortise' with sloping shoulders. The joint is secured by means of string or wire passing through holes drilled as shown. Such a joint allows almost full flexion in one direction and negligible movement in the other. The looseness of the fit also allows a natural movement in the opposite plane.

The second leg is made by fastening leather joints at the knee and ankle with their edges towards the front of the body. Thin wire nails allow the limbs to swivel adequately, and a piece of thread tied to the back of the upper and lower legs provides a 'stop' to prevent the knee bending the wrong way. The parts of the leg should be shaped so that they engage closely but do not restrict movement.

The last example is a simple knee joint with a cut-away at the back to allow a generous bend. The hinge is a

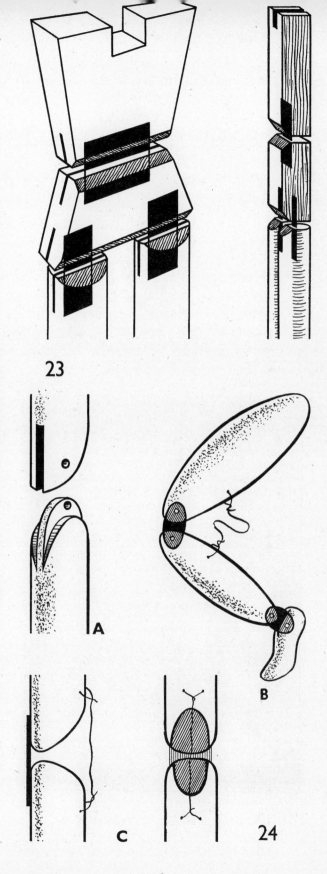

23

A

B

C

24

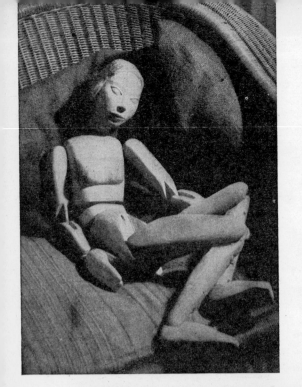

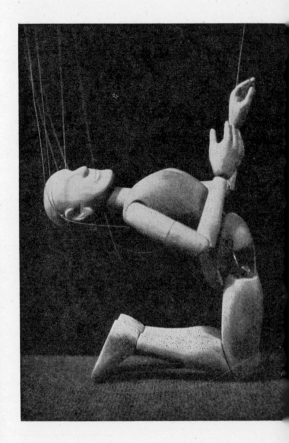

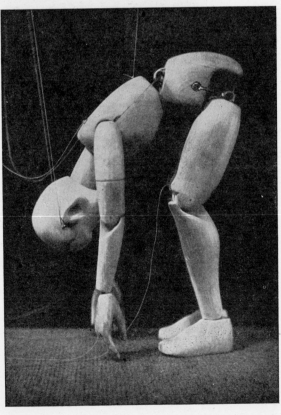

Waldo S. Lanchester: *on this page and opposite, above*, five figures illustrating the mechanics of a typical Lanchester creation.

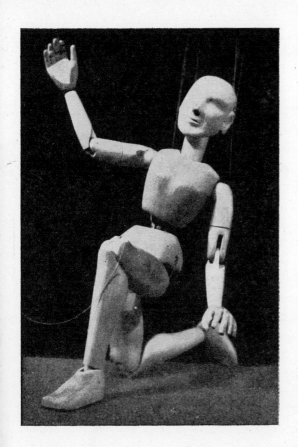

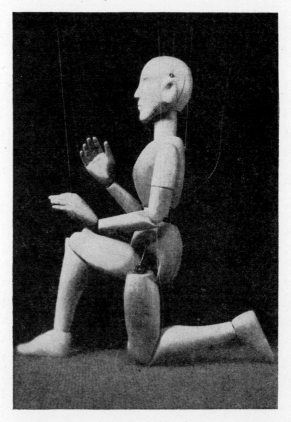

Right: a wooden marionette
turned on the lathe by Jan Malik.
Photo: V. Scholz.

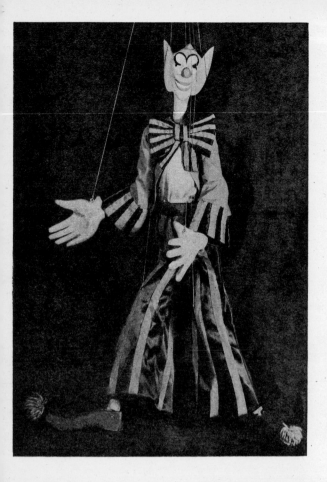

Kenneth Wood: a clown. Note the hands and feet which are made of heavy wood to give breadth of swing in clown-like movements. The arms, from shoulder to elbow, are made of string, weighted at the elbow. The lines of the face are cut well back to throw the features into bold relief.

piece of thin leather glued at the front, and this joint, too, has a check made of thread.

HANDS

The hands illustrated in figure 25 each have points to commend them.

A dowel 'cuff' on the first is fastened to the arm with thin leather strips, and has a piece of wire of hand-shape attached to it, upon which the actual hand can be modelled in papier mâché or Plasticine covered with pasted paper.

Old curtain wire of the expanding type is used in the second. Both hand and cuff are made from dowel rod and have holes drilled down the centre of each in which a length of curtain wire can be glued. Before attaching the hand, take a piece out with a saw as illustrated, and finish to shape with a pen-knife and glasspaper. The wire allows free movement, but the edge of the hand dowel, engaging with the end of the arm, prevents unwanted backward flexion.

Finally, as shown in figure 25 the normal screw-eye joint can be improved with a leather check. It is indeed a good plan to fix two checks, one below and one above the wrist.

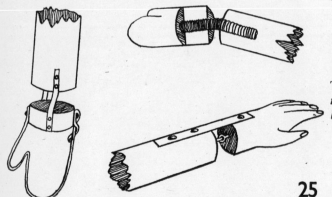

Types of hands. *Left*: wire frame with dowel cuff; *top right*: curtain wire allows for easy flexion; *bottom right*: leather check prevents full movement.

25

John Wright's Marionettes: Briar Rose and Prince Charming from *Briar Rose* by Rose Fyleman.

12. SPECIALITIES

To say the novel effects which can be achieved with marionettes are almost limitless is scarcely an overstatement.

All marionette-makers find themselves collecting apparently useless odds and ends. Buttons, cotton-reels, odd pieces of material, wire, beads, instead of being thrown away or hidden in the box-room, will find their way into a special box. And it is from this box that the ideas for novelty marionettes will, perhaps unconsciously, develop to the stage that you just *have* to make them.

In describing the amusing characters who came to life in this way, I do not pretend they are particularly original. They do, however, illustrate how seemingly uninteresting scrap materials may sometimes have interesting possibilities to the marionette enthusiast.

SAMMY THE SNAKE

Sammy began as a collection of old cotton reels. These suggested some kind of multi-jointed body, and a snake was the rather obvious answer.

These were strung together with a bead between each reel to allow smooth articulation. Now only the head and tail were needed.

The head was made from an old piece of felt cut to the pattern shown and with a wire tongue covered with red flannel. The eyes were black shoe buttons with a dab of white enamel at the centre. The tail was made from a wallpaper bead.

The control was designed to give the movement needed, and a short length of bamboo cane with strings to the cotton-reels at intervals on the body provided the solution. In performance, the snake with this form of control is held *just clear* of the stage floor in order to facilitate movement. Sammy does not roll over the stage as the wriggle does *not* involve any rotation of the cotton reels. He was given a continuous stripe of green paint, which made him seem almost as sinuous as a real snake.

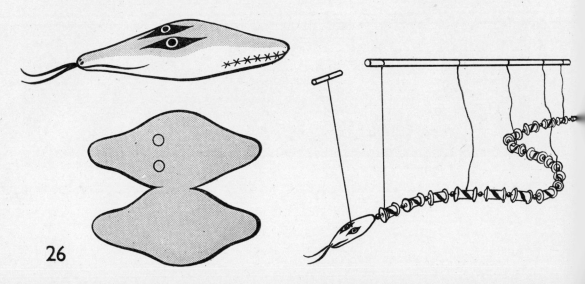

Anglo-Austrian Puppet Theatre ostrich on a tightrope. Photo: Juliet Haddon, St Albans.

Gair Wilkinson's *St George and the Dragon*: the rescue of Princess Cleodolinda from the dragon's claws.

EGBERT THE OSTRICH

This is an example of what can be done with such apparently unrelated items as an old wooden ball, a length of gas mask tubing, some feathers and scrap plywood. I was introduced to him at the Pioneer Palace in Leningrad.

The head is modelled in papier mâché and has a beak made from a piece of carved wood inserted before the head is dry. The gas mask tubing makes a beautifully supple neck which is tacked to the wooden body.

The legs are cut from plywood, and pivot on a bolt going right through the ball. The feathers are sewn to a leather pad which is then glued on the body. Wire covered with adhesive tape provides the feet.

The wings can be moved by vibrating the controls.

Egbert can also do almost incredible things with his head.

Perhaps his walk is rather clumsy, but when strung as shown, his antics will cause considerable amusement.

THE JUGGLER

This trick marionette is included to show what can be done with special stringing. Special function strings enable marionettes to perform successful tricks even in the hands of a relative novice. They instil a confidence in manipulation which arises from the fact that the marionette simply cannot do the wrong thing. The Juggler is one of these fool-proof models. Whereas the real-life juggler must always have at the back of his mind the awful possibility of a fluffed trick, our marionette juggler can only drop the ball in the unlikely event of a broken string.

Choose a large wooden ball, and drill a generous hole down the centre. Smooth the inside with a piece of glasspaper wound round a knitting needle. Through this hole, thread the hand strings, and attach to a control bar about 6 inches long.

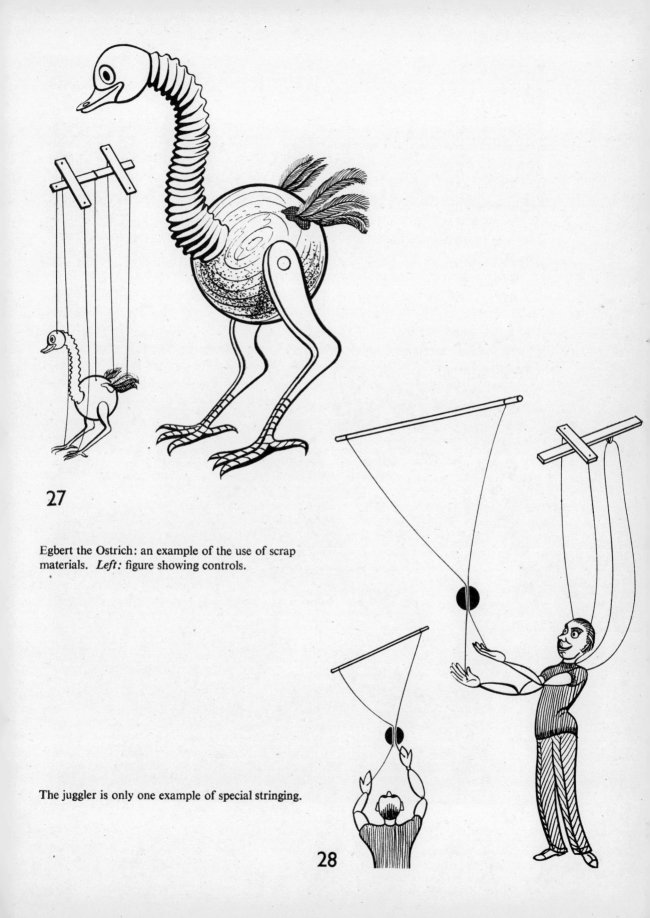

27

Egbert the Ostrich: an example of the use of scrap
materials. *Left:* figure showing controls.

The juggler is only one example of special stringing.

28

The hands should be large and flat, with the controls passing upwards through the palms.

When the right-hand tip of the control is raised, the Juggler lifts his right hand and the ball therefore rests on it, figure 28.

To transfer the ball to the other hand, flick up the right hand tip of the control. The jerk of the marionette's hand under the ball will send it up the string. Now gently raise the left hand tip of the control. This brings up the Juggler's left hand to the ball. A little practice and you have a realistic but extremely simple act.

The Juggler is only one example of a marionette which will give a most effective turn in your theatre. There are many other examples of foolproof stringing. Decide what you want your puppet to do, and arrange the strings accordingly. In this way you can easily make trapeze artists who never miss the trapeze (because their hand strings are threaded through it), marionettes who can balance sticks on their hands or heads, and other similar circus turns.

This feature of marionette work relies almost entirely on the way the marionettes are made and strung. It is the simplest way of producing an effect which will quite literally amaze as well as amuse audiences. The puppeteer's work is three-quarters done before his creation first steps on the stage. The rest is easy.

Anglo-Austrian Puppet Theatre: Tyrolese yodeller.

Figure 29: a device for obtaining a realistic walk—the rocker lifts the legs alternately.

Opposite: Waldo S. Lanchester's Monsieur Pataluski.

A REALISTIC WALK

The walk of a marionette is usually the least satisfactory feature of even the most skilfully-made models, and many puppeteers have experimented with devices of their own in an attempt to remedy this defect.

One such device, which gives excellent results in practised hands, is illustrated here. It is the combined invention of Geoffrey Holme and the late George Sheringham.

The important detail is that the hips are made in two oval sections glued to a central spine and about an inch apart. The upper legs are fastened with screw-eyes to short wooden pieces which slide freely in holes cut out of the ovals. Each piece has two stops made from dowel pins, one ¼ inch above the upper oval and the other ¼ inch beneath the lower.

When the leg control attached to the top of the wooden piece is rocked, one leg is raised until checked by the stop pin, and the body is moved forward, leaving the other leg in contact with the floor. The swinging leg is then dropped. This movement is repeated with the opposite leg.

A little practice will enable you, by moving the body smoothly forward, and, at the same time, rocking the lever controlling these movable legs, to produce a good semblance of the human walk.

73

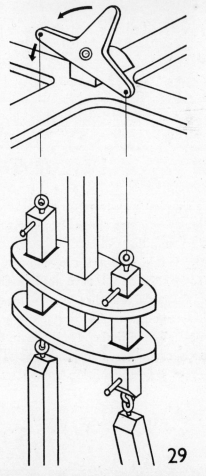

29

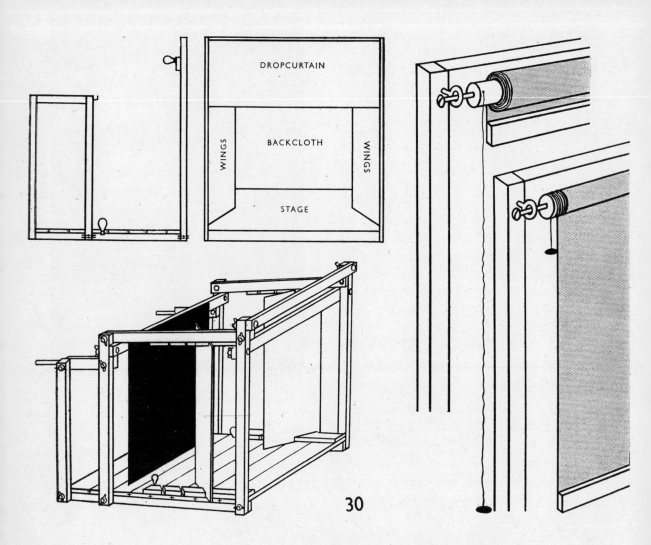

DROPCURTAIN

WINGS

BACKCLOTH

WINGS

STAGE

30

13.   A SIMPLE THEATRE

The simplest way to make a marionette theatre is to drape a curtain across an open doorway or over a clothes-horse and to use the drawing-room carpet as your stage.

Although this will help you to become used to working a marionette when it is only partly visible, several shortcomings will be revealed, and a special theatre be needed.

To be effective this need not be elaborate, and the design given here can be simplified even further if your theatre is to be a temporary affair and portability is not required.

To make a complete portable theatre such as illustrated in figure 30 you will need some 38 feet of timber $1 \times \frac{1}{2}$–1 inch, 17 feet of 2×1 inch, 12 4-inch boards or 8 6-inch boards, each 4 feet 6 inches long and preferably $\frac{1}{2}$ inch thick, and a piece of lath 4 feet 6 inches long. In addition, some strawboard for the wings, an old sheet or curtain for the canopy and curtains are wanted, together with 20 butterfly nuts and bolts and some screw-eyes and hooks. The minimum of tools includes a saw, hammer, some 2-inch screws, a screwdriver and a drill.

CONSTRUCTION

To make the stage, saw two pieces of 2×1 inch timber each to a length of 4 feet.

Take your 4 feet 6 inch boards, preferably of the match-boarding type, and screw the ends to the 2×1 inch pieces, making a covered platform. To the sides of this platform the remaining parts of the theatre, made from the smaller timber, are fastened with butterfly nuts and bolts as shown in figure 30.

Two pieces 5 feet long at the front corner, joined across the top by a 4 feet $\times$ 6 inch length, complete the proscenium arch. At the back on either side a frame is fitted, and supported across the centre with a further piece 4 feet 6 inches in length.

To complete the theatre, bolt a piece of lath to the back of the proscenium arch about 9 inches from the top: when fitted with lamp-holders this acts as a lighting strip. The bulbs should be shielded to make full use of this illumination. Bent tin can be used for these masks.

Cut two wings, approximately 4 feet 6 inches $\times$ 9 inches, from strawboard. These are tacked or screwed to the wing supports. Four pieces of lath, sawn through diagonally in two or three places, and glued to either side of the stage, top and bottom, with sufficient gaps to take the edge of the strawboard, provide a convenient means of sliding-in the wings.

Screw hooks to the front of the back frame for the backcloths, and further hooks inside the sidepieces of the same frame on which to hang the marionettes when not performing.

Backcloth illumination is provided by bulbs let into the stage floor just in front of the back framework. The wiring is concealed beneath the stage itself. Shields of bent tin should be used to screen these from the audience.

There are several alternative methods of fixing and operating curtains. One of the best is to use a roller curtain, mounted on a piece of $\frac{1}{2}$-inch dowel and hung *in front* of the proscenium. The dowel should be assembled with a 'stop' to prevent the thread winding off when the curtain is being operated. This stop can be a small piece of shaped plywood or a cotton-reel glued to the end of the dowel rod. The lower edge of the curtain has a weighted batten fastened across.

After rolling up the curtain, drill a hole through the end of the dowel and thread with thin cord. When the curtain is unrolled, the cord winds round the dowel and can be used to pull the curtain up again. For clarity this is shown in the diagram without the stop in position. Attachment to the proscenium is by means of a round-headed screw in the end of the dowel which slips through a large screw-eye in the proscenium frame.

If you wish to hang the curtain behind the proscenium framework, attach it to the

wooden blocks holding the lighting strip. It is now necessary to make a proscenium arch from strawboard or plywood in order to cover the exposed top of the theatre. This should also be done if you decide to fit draw curtains instead of the roller type described here.

Drop curtains may be a little less ' theatrical ' but they have one distinct advantage. Whatever the height of the stage, they can be adjusted to screen the puppeteers from the view of the audience.

To further screen the operators, and to keep distracting shadows off the ceiling, fasten an old sheet or curtain to the top corners of the proscenium frame and tie above the back of the stage. The sides of the theatre can be screened in the same way.

The complete theatre should be placed on a stout table, in which case the performers stand on the stage behind the backcloth. If you have two tables, so much the better. You can dispense with the back framework and reduce the dimensions of the stage accordingly. Choose the lower of the two tables for the stage and stand on the other, which is placed against it. This gives a few extra inches height and makes control easier. You will now need to make a backcloth frame resting on the floor and lashed or clamped to the back table for support.

The measurements given here are quite arbitrary and should be adjusted to suit individual requirements. Any successful marionette theatre will, however, need a framework something like this model and, with increasing skill on the part of the performers,

Opposite: the backcloth which provides a setting for the finale of Carlo Gozzi's *Deer King*, Moscow Puppet Theatre (see page 28). After many trials and tribulations all ends happily and the lovers are reunited.

Between shows the puppets should be kept in a bag as a protection against dust and the possibility of the strings being caught up. The quickest, and in fact the only, way to deal with a stubborn tangle is to cut the controls and completely re-string. Photo: Anglo-Austrian Puppet Theatre.

there will come a demand for more and more height and size for the operating platform.

This can be temporarily solved by raising the back framework and providing boxes on which to stand, but when this is no longer adequate, your troupe is clearly ready for a more elaborate theatre.

If you are fortunate enough to have an unwanted kitchen table, you can economise in timber by using this as the stage, and fastening your various frames direct to it. For several reasons, however, portability is generally to be recommended, and this can further be increased by making the frames collapsible. The simplest joints for this purpose are made by driving two nails into the ends of the cross timbers, and removing the heads with cutting pliers. These improvised bolts then slip through corresponding holes drilled at the top of the side pieces.

Be sure to stow all electrical wiring out of sight. If necessary, drill holes in the side pieces of the proscenium frame to take strings with which to lash the wires tight to the woodwork.

One final refinement worth mentioning is that, if you have a large cast in your marionette show, a piece of dowel rod attached to the back of the framework will help considerably. The marionettes are hung on this in the order that they will be needed in the show. When they have made their exit, transfer them to the hooks on the side frame with the bodies hanging outside the stage, out of harm's way.

BACKCLOTHS AND FURNITURE

Backcloths can be as simple or detailed as the play demands. Curtaining draped over the backcloth frame will serve for individual turns. Scenic backcloths will need to be designed to meet the needs of your particular play, but even here, it is as well to err on the side of simplicity.

First, decide upon a scale-size to suit your marionettes: since these are made first and are the most important factors in your theatre, everything else is made to accommodate and enhance them. Scenery is painted on paper backcloths fastened with Bulldog clips at each side to a 'master' frame which is made from strawboard and hangs by two hooks from the rear framework of the theatre.

As with the live theatre, scenery is painted to give the *appearance* of realism under stage-lighting conditions. Detail is often wasted, and may even draw the attention of the audience away from the marionettes, so keep your effects bold and use poster colours.

Solid scenery, such as tables and chairs, should be kept to a minimum to allow your puppets free movement about the stage. Small items, which can be easily knocked over, should be secured to the stage by improvised drop bolts of the type described for use with a portable stage framework. This device also assists quick arrangement when changing scenes, and small holes in the stage flooring are invisible to an audience.

LIGHTING

Take skilled advice on the matter of lighting. All lights should be accommodated in proper holders and should be well clear of anything inflammable. They should also be shielded to prevent breakage to the bulbs as well as throwing the light in the required direction. This apart, lighting has considerable possibilities in achieving special effects, and here coloured bulbs may be used to advantage. For simplicity, there is no better way than tying a torch covered with coloured paper to the theatre framework when required.

If you have that sort of skill, it is possible to fit your theatre with a comprehensive stage lighting set, complete with rheostat, coloured slides and a control box.

However, for all but 'professional' performances, nothing more elaborate than the lighting strip and backcloth-illumination described here are necessary.

This theatre will provide your home-made marionettes with an adequate world in which to exercise their newly-won skills before a sympathetic audience.

STORING MARIONETTES

If you find yourself with the task of unravelling the tangled strings of a marionette, you will appreciate to the full any means of preventing a recurrence. When not actually performing on the stage, they should be hung by the hook at the end of the control bar.

Between shows, they are best kept in a cloth bag with a drawstring. Make a bag to fit each marionette, and, after winding the hand strings round the hand control, slip over the body and draw tight. If possible, hang in a cupboard by the control.

14. TO THE FUTURE

The organisation of a marionette theatre is scarcely less complex than that of its live counterpart. In addition to stage management, lighting, music and sound effects, there is the actual manipulation of the marionettes to be considered, and highly developed teamwork is necessary to put on a large-scale show.

The present general appeal of the marionette theatre is only sufficient to support a handful of professional artists, and, unfortunately, there is little official financial support from sources by which the development of a national marionette tradition can be assisted. When one considers the tremendous possibilities of the marionette theatre as a cultural and educational medium, this seems little short of tragic.

Those puppeteers who, despite lack of support, pursue the path of artistic integrity, deserve high praise. Fortunately, there are signs that their efforts are meeting with a growing response.

You may well find that your marionettes lend themselves most readily to the music hall turn. I hope this will not discourage you from attempting more ambitious work with your troupe. The ballads, legends and traditional stories of Britain and other countries offer unrivalled scope for sympathetic interpretation through puppetry. They also extend the range of the theatre to include scenery and lighting as an integral part of the production.

A permanent marionette theatre may one day be a feature of the majority of our schools. I can think of no other way in which such a tremendous range of skills can be incorporated into one project. It offers, in miniature, the whole field of drama, but, in addition, the making and clothing of the marionettes and the building of the theatre.

These, in turn, lead to practical work in craft, stage-lighting, and to research into historical costume. There is also the writing of scripts, scene-painting and the actual operation of the marionettes. For every degree and type of skill there is something to do.

I hope that the practical details of marionette construction collected together in this book may assist in some small way the development of latent artistry and skills towards the realisation of a new and exciting phase in the story of the marionette theatre.

A short list of books will be found overleaf; they cover most branches of puppetry for those—and there will be many—who, having gone thus far, will wish to explore to the full the fascinating possibilities of this art.

BIBLIOGRAPHY

The following books are recommended by the Educational Puppetry Association.

GENERAL AND HISTORICAL

Beaumont, C. W.   *Puppets and the Puppet Stage*   Studio, 1938
Boehn, Max von   *Dolls and Puppets*   Harrap, 1932
Joseph, Helen H.   *A Book of Marionettes*   New York
Puppeteers of America   *Puppetry*   Detroit,   Annually

CONSTRUCTION

Bussell, Jan   *The Puppet Theatre*   Faber, 1946
Green, Dana S.   *Masks and Puppets*   Studio, 1942
Lanchester, Waldo S.   *Hand Puppets and String Puppets*   Dryad, 1938
Rossbach, Edmund   *Making Marionettes*   Harcourt, Brace, 1938
Whanslaw, H. W.   *Everybody's Marionette Book*   Wells Gardner, 1924

PLAYS FOR MARIONETTES

Hamburg Puppet Guild (USA)   *Dancing Dolls*   French, 1937
Kreymborg, A.   *Puppet Plays*   Secker, 1923
McPharlin, Paul   *Ed.*   *Repertory of Marionette Plays*   New York, Viking Press, 1929
Whanslaw, H. W.   *Book of Marionette Plays*   Wells Gardner

W. Schwerzmann's head of The Doctor from *Der Schatz in der Truhe*
(*The Treasure Chest*) by Jacob Flach (1948): Marionettentheater, Ascona.